DEVELOPMENT OF CREATIVITY IN INDIAN SCHOOLS

ABOUT THE AUTHOR

DR. K.P. AGARWAL, after completing his M.Sc. (Modern Mathematics) and M.Ed. from Aligarh Muslim University, did his Ph.D. in Education from Jamia Millia Islamia, New Delhi under the supervision of Prof. Baqer Mehdi. Dr. Agarwal is teaching in Education Department, N.R.E.C. College, Khurja affiliated to Meerut University. He has participated in a number of conferences and seminars for the innovation of Education and for the nurturance of Creativity among school children. Having done a lot of work in creativity in Indian schools, he is, at present, actively associated in imparting education to the would be teachers of the countrry, broadening their attitude to love and encourage the human groping behaviour and stressing on accountability, character formation and moral values.

DEVELOPMENT OF CREATIVITY IN INDIAN SCHOOLS

Some Related Issues

K.P. AGARWAL
Department of Education, N.R.E.C. College
Khurja

CONCEPT PUBLISHING COMPANY, NEW DELHI 110059

The Indian Council of Social Science Research gave the financial support towards the publication of this work. However, the responsibility for the contents of the book — facts, opinions, conclusions, etc. — is entirely that of the author and not of the ICSSR.

ICSSR Consultant: DR. R.C. SHARMA

ISBN 81-7022-430-6

First Published 1992

Published and Printed by
Ashok Kumar Mittal
Concept Publishing Company
A/15-16, Commercial Block, Mohan Garden
NEW DELHI 110059 (India)

Lasertypeset by
Microtech Advance Printing Systems (Pvt.) Ltd.
H-13, Bali Nagar,
NEW DELHI 110015

Where the mind is without fear,
  and the head is held high;
Where knowledge is free;
Where the world has not been broken up into fragments
  by narrow domestic walls;
Where words come out from the depth of truth;
Where tireless striving stretches its arms
  towards perfection;
Where the mind is led forward by thee
  into ever-widening thought and action –
Into that heaven of freedom,
  my Father,
  let my country awake.

— Ravindranath Tagore *Geetanjali*

DEDICATED

to

Those who sacrificed for the sake of humanity.

My parents and teachers who loved me a lot and inspired me for higher studies.

FOREWORD

There has been a considerable awareness about education at various levels in India. Recently, the Government of India constituted a Committee called the Acharya Ramamurti Committee to review the National Policy of Education (NPE), 1986. This Committee, after a series of meetings, finalized its report and submitted to the Government. Some of the salient features of this report are as follows:

1. The most important agency for education is considered to be the school and it is in the school that the entire personality of a child develops. It is in the schools that both formal and non-formal education take place. The Committee has recommended that school education should be made universal.
2. The second important recommendation made by the Committee is that education should be made more creative bringing in vocation into the system. All essential resources, both financial and intellectual, should be made available to the schools to enable it to reach out to the children including girls. The school should open-up and non-formalize education in creative ways.

In the light of these recommendations, the thesis submitted by Dr. Kanta Prasad Agarwal, in candidature for the degree of Ph.D. of Jamia Millia Islamia, becomes very relevant. The title of the thesis is *Types of Schools and Corresponding Factors as Predictors of Creativity at Secondary Level*. In his studies, the author has collected data on different types of schools and has pointed out what are the constraints towards creativity. Researches in the field of creativity indicate that the potential for creativity in a child is the first necessary step towards developing his ability and personality. Dr. Agarwal's researches identify the various forms of creativity. He has also drawn our attention to the types of schools and the classroom learning environment. His observations on the school-wise creativity levels of students are very interesting and important. He also indicates the relationship between teacher's perception and creativity. Finally, he identifies the socio-economic status of students. He has made studies in different types of schools and has given a relationship between socio-economic status and creativity.

Thus the work of Dr. Kanta Prasad Agarwal is indeed valuable and would be of much interest to teachers, educationists and planners involved in the administration and management of education in the country.

Jamia Millia Islamia-Central University
Jamia Nagar
New Delhi 110025

S.Z. QASIM
Vice Chancellor

PREFACE

The world's achievements in every period are shaped by creative abilities of talented persons. The milestones of human history were installed by creative achievements in the past. Not only the material advancement but also the progress in art and literature, scientific discoveries and evolution of dynamic, social and political orders have been the contribution of creative persons.

Historical records provide evidence that cultures have collapsed because of the failure to utilise the creative power of their people.

The educational activities at school remained very much centred around the development of convergent thinking with almost a total neglect of nurturing to divergent thinking abilities and skills. It is this dissatisfaction with the present classroom teaching and environment, as a teacher as well as a teacher-educator that led me to the present problem.

Though the book is a result of my doctoral study, it is primarily intended to benefit research scholars, school and college teachers who can help the children in many ways – particularly those children whose creativity remains stifled.

The book is concerned with creativity levels in different types of schools namely Aided, Government, Kendriya and Public; and how does the school environment affect creative achievements. The book also focuses on the role of teachers in creativity development of students by studying teachers' perceptions about ideal pupil. The book also studies the relationship of socio-economic status with creativity.

It is my proud privilege to express my indebtedness, deep sense of gratitude and hearty thanks to Prof. Baqer Mehdi, NCERT, New Delhi for enlightened guidance and encouragement in the completion of this work.

This study owes much to the generosity, friendship and guidance of many individuals, institutions and organisations throughout this country and abroad. I am grateful to Prof. K.G. Sharma, Meerut

University, Prof. R.C. Deva, A.M.U. Aligarh, Prof. N.K. Jangira, Prof. M.K. Raina, Prof. R.K. Mathur of NCERT, New Delhi, Prof. Dr. (Mrs.) Purnima Mathur, I.I.T., New Delhi, N.K. Nijhawan, Director, Data Archives, S.P. Agrawal, Former Director, Documentation Centre, ICSSR, New Delhi, my colleague, late Shri S.C. Sharma and Dr. Rajeev Lochan, N.R.E.C. College, Khurja for their valuable suggestions, help and encouragement in the completion of the work.

I am greatly indebted to Dr. E. Paul Torrance, University of Georgia, U.S.A., and Dr. Barry J. Fraser, Macquarie University, Sydney, Australia for their generosity in sending the required research materials to me.

I also feel delighted in mentioning the name of my wife Smt. Daya Rani, son Kumar Gaurav, lovely daughters Km. Himani and Smita for giving me help and cooperation in my work.

I express my deep indebtness and sincere regards to my parents and teachers who have been a source of constant inspiration, encouragement and warmth in my higher studies.

In the end, I am grateful to Prof. S.Z. Qasim, Vice-Chancellor of Jamia Millia Islamia for writing Foreword of the work.

My thanks are also due to the ICSSR, New Delhi for providing financial support for the publication of the work.

K.P. AGARWAL
Department of Education
N.R.E.C. College,
Khurja

Chetra Purnima, 2049 Vikrami
17 April, 1992

CONTENTS

LIST OF TABLES

1

INTRODUCTION

"Imagination is more important than knowledge."

—*Albert Einstein*

The level of development of a nation is directly proportional to the identification of talent, its nurturing and optimal utilisation. Most of the advanced countries have recognised this fact and have taken steps for the identification and nurturing the talent. In the case of underdeveloped countries the situation is otherwise. Rousseau laments gross neglect of the creative talent: "In every underdeveloped country potential Einstein and Fords are herding cattle or breaking stones" (Rousseau, 1962).

In our own country one finds impressive manpower in quantitative as well as qualitative terms when the baseline level at the time of Independence is taken into consideration. If our aspirations are to match those of the advanced nations, pursuit of excellence is the only alternative. The pursuit of excellence as a goal can be realised only when we develop a system for identification and nurturing of talent right from early stages of the development of the child.

To turn each potential individual into competent and high principled citizen is an urgent necessity. The solution of our problems of growth and development lie in providing a type of education to our children which will enable them to think intelligently and creatively. The questions before, us, then, are: Can we train our children who can find original solutions to new problems? Can we produce leaders who realise the uniqueness of nation's problems and find unique solutions for the betterment and prosperity of the country? The task before the educator, therefore, is to identify, encourage and develop creative talent in order to survive and progress in the international competition.

In our society many old traditions have given place to new ones.

We welcome newness in certain walks of life. Unfortunately we seldom look for such a newness in our education and in our teaching-learning process. As Guilford (1962) puts it, "If we are ready to tolerate the idea of drastic changes, we are not ready for an age of creative education".

Maslow (1954), while observing the perpetual and fast change in the history of man, goes to the extent of saying: ". . . what is the use of teaching facts? Facts become obsolete and so darned fast. What is the use of teaching techniques? They too become obsolete so fast. They should give up teaching of the tried and true methods of the past in favour of trying to create a new kind of human being who is comfortable with change, who enjoys change, who is able to improvise, who is able to face with confidence, strength and courage a situation of which he has absolutely no fore-warning."

Education so far has emphasised abilities only in the area of convergent thinking and evaluation often at the expense of development in the area of divergent thinking. We have attempted to teach students how to arrive at correct answers, but have not cared to develop the ability to ask intelligent questions and answer them creatively.

Bloom (1958) is very pessimistic about development of creativity among the learners through the present school set-up. He says: "There is some reason to believe that the educational system as it prevails today can reduce originality and creativity. This negative effect on creativity is most marked when examinations, instructional materials and processes all emphasise learning by rote and the goal is centered on getting through examinations."

Modern education must therefore not content itself with developing mere rote learning but also the ability of children to produce relevant new meanings of their class-room experiences. It is obligatory on the part of the school to equip the child with generalised intellectual and other skills which will enable him to cope effectively with whatever state of the world he will encounter later in life. The most important of these generalised skills is creative thinking. The greatest joy of the teacher and the greatest hope for a better world lies in the cultivation of creative power. "To teach towards creativity is to teach towards the future of society". (Lowenfeld and Brittain, 1966).

The plain fact is that there is a need for nurturing creativity in every school. Wherever it is done, it is by chance and accident rather than by design and understanding. A Review Committee (1977) appointed by the Government of India pointed out the distortion that has crept into our educational system. The Review Committee observed that the general conditions prevailing in the majority of our schools progressively reduce the urge to experiment and to undertake creative work.

In the concluding remark the Review Committee has emphasised the need of creative education without mincing words. It maintains:

> If the purpose of education is to nurture the child's capacities to the full and to give our people not only a useful occupation but a full and abundant life, then the creative urge in the children must in every possible way be actively stimulated and cultivated in as many directions as possible.

Need and Importance of the Study

School is the only place where perhaps an organised effort can be made to ensure a continuous flow of trained intellect.

Unfortunately, the organisation of our schools, our curricula, our text books and our teaching methods pay homage to what Osborn (1963) said, the same 'God of conformity'.

It is but natural to expect in such a situation that the urge to enquire, to invent and to experiment is curbed in the millions of our school children resulting in the death of creative spark.

Torrance (1969) is of the view that if waste of human talent is to be prevented and if creatively gifted students are not to choose the paths of delinquency, mental illness or at best a life of mediocrity and unrealised potentialities, it becomes undoubtedly essential that serious attempts are made towards measurement of factors which would determine creativity.

As is generally observed, many students seem to possess the seeds of creativeness but the environment fails to provide full nourishment for their growth.

Thus the assessment of a broad range of predictor variables is needed to determine the best combination of predictors at all stages of children education. Of the different educational levels the intermediate (Senior Secondary Years) has been the most neglected stage in creativity research.

Gupta (1974) surveyed the field of creativity in India and found projects in various stages of completion as mentioned in the Table 1.1.

TABLE 1.1: Classification of Indian Researches on Creativity in Major Fields. (1974)

	Field of Creativity	No. of Studies
1.	Process	26
2.	Relation to personality	29
3.	Relation to achievement and other variables	7
4.	Creative environment	6
5.	Creative product	3
6.	Miscellaneous	5

It is apparent from the table that the majority of research has been done in the area of personality as related to creativity, while other important areas as creative environment still remain to be fully investigated.

The aim of the present study, therefore, is to suggest desirable changes which must be brought about in the learning environment to create conducive climate in the classroom so that it may be best shifted for nurturing the creative talents of pupils which have remained almost neglected so far in our schools.

Thus the present investigation is undertaken to seek the answer of the following questions: How classroom environment is related with creativity? Can it be developed among our pupils while they are at school? What factors underlie such a development? What implications it has for modifying the classroom climate/environment of the schools and behaviour of teachers to facilitate creativity?

Since very few studies are available on environmental factors conducive to the development of creativity, there is very little yet known through research about environmental settings that are ideal for the promotion of creativity. For example, there is no relevant study available which might have attempted to investigate the comparative levels of creativity in students from various types of schools and corresponding factors as predictors of creativity in students of these schools. This has provided the necessary motivation to the present investigator to conduct the study.

Statement of the Problem

The purpose of this investigation is to examine the possible involvement of classroom environment and teachers' attitude into creative achievement of secondary level male students. The different types of schools whose Socio-emotional climates have been studied in the present investigation are: (i) Private Aided Schools, (ii) Government Schools, (iii) Kendriya Vidyalayas, and (iv) Public Schools. Specifically the problem can be stated as:

> "Types of Schools and Corresponding Factors as Predictors of Creativity at Secondary Level".

In the remaining part of the chapter, an attempt will be made to broadly discuss the importance of environment to the development of creative learning abilities.

Environment and Learning

Behaviour is the resultant of two interdependent vectors — person and environment — operating in a dynamic field of 'Life Space' (Lewin, 1936). Brunswik (1957) suggested that all aspects of the geographic-historic-physical environment are potentially relevant to learning. Walberg (1970) stated that much of the reliable variance in student performance is attributable to the aptitude of the learner and the environment of learning. Research on the teaching-learning process should provide for analysis of aptitude and environment and their interactions with instruction.

In view of the importance of environment as manipulable factor in learning, the locus of interest in educational measurement is beginning to shift from measures of the individual to measures of the environment. Environmental assessments may make it possible:

(a) to improve the accuracy of predicting learning, and
(b) to manipulate the environment to bring out optimal conditions of learning (Walberg, 1969b).

The learning environment may be present in the school, home, and community. Of these the school produces the first and perhaps the most insistent and subtle influence on the mental ability development of the child.

Environment and Creativity

There is strong evidence which indicates that creativity does not just happen. The conditions for creativity will have to be carefully nourished if we want more creativity to be demonstrated (Hilgard, 1959; Torrance, 1962; Murphy, 1966). The propitious environment for creativity is the 'Open System' (Anderson, 1962). As distinguished from a "Closed System", openness designates those characteristics of the environment, both the inner and the outer, the personal and the social, which facilitate the creative person's moving from the actual state of affairs which he is in at a given time toward solutions which are only possible and as yet undetermined (Hallman, 1963). Children can be helped to inculcate and preserve such characteristics and conditions and thereby develop creativity by non-authoritarian attitudes on the part of parents and teachers and by providing a responsive environment. A responsive environment means "building an atmosphere of receptive listening, relieving the fears of the overtaught and over-guided, fending off devastating disparagement and criticism, stirring the sluggish and deepening the superficial, making sure that every sincere effort brings enough satisfaction to assure continued effort, heightening sensory awareness and keeping alive the zest for learning and thinking." (Torrance, 1963). Such approaches are typified by O.K. Moore's (1961) "Responsive environment" in which children are propelled by their own curiosity, the adult or the environment only responding promptly to the child's efforts to learn. A much more ambitious environment has been created by Karlins and Schroder (1967).The nurturant environment both at home and in school is one which gives a free reign and a ready response to the explorations of the child.

Creative potentialities unmask themselves in an 'Open System' of Education and flourish in a 'responsive' and 'stimulating' environment. The death Knell to creativity is rung in a school where environment is surcharged by conformity, rigidity, strict obedience and traditionalism (Goyal, 1973).

Classroom and Creativity

Children have the ambivalent feeling of wanting to destroy and needing to repair or restore, and if we hope to foster creativity we must first and foremost allow them the freedom to explore this potentially fruitful tension. An environment which allows children to express both negative and positive feelings, to experiment and discover and to act independently and responsibly provides the ideal preparations.

If a child comes to school unencumbered by excess weight of conflict from the home, such a free exploration of his own powers will be much easier.

Only if he is given the freedom to explore his inner conflicts in a safe environment which supports the ego in its demanding task of discovery will be able to begin to muster repressed inner energies for truly constructive purposes. If such a learning environment is not provided, then the very least we can expect is continuing rigidity and repression; at worst, the child's hostile feelings will eventually break through in some form of destructive behaviour.

Can the inhabitants of a classroom convey a sense of wonder, discovery and concern in their daily lives together? It would seem that they must share a sense of closeness with one another. The classroom atmosphere must be illuminated by a sense of love and respect. Eble (1968) would agree: "To learn is to love. Any sound education must grow from this principle-which does not permit itself to be a principle, but instead an understanding".

Members would play and work together in a happy, rationally permissive manner and by confronting the unknown as well as the comfortably familiar together, learners would recognise the twin needs of freedom and order in any undertaking. Singly or in a team, students would quest after the solution of stimulating problems in unique, relevant and satisfying learning experiences. Sir Herbert Read cites the importance of cooperation in his definition of the creative classroom.

The classroom then would evolve as a place where each would be in a communion with all. A genuine community of mutuals sharing would result in which each would be "opened up and drawn in. . . . Freedom in education is the possibility of communion" (Buber, 1961).

High schoolers conducting a community survey on water pollution spend many hours beyond class time. The sense of team work, a sharpened understanding of community pressures, the ever new experiences of confrontation with other human beings all occur in an atmosphere of comradeship while young people are walking and driving around their own community.

In exhorting educators to adopt more encouraging approaches towards inquiry and problem solving, Wiesner (1968) states: "It is important, especially in childhood and early youth, that novel ideas and unconventional patterns of action should be more widely tolerated and not criticised too soon and too often."

We must allow students the freedom to be, to become their best selves. Inquiring individuals and aware members of an ever widening community need some permissiveness.

The permissiveness which is being described is not softness or indulgence or encouragement. It is permission to be free, which also means that one is responsible (Rogers, 1970).

Following a study of the informal versus formal English schools, Haddon and Lytton (1970) concluded:

> It is certainly not permissiveness which is the distinguishing criterion of informality as opposed to formality. The most striking difference lies in the degree of emphasis in the informal schools and fundamental to its success, lies the pattern of interpersonal relationship within the school.

Will a creative classroom where the unexpected, the novel, and even gaiety are found be a productive learning environment? Torrance (1969) who feels that creative approaches are both preferable and beneficial gives many suggestions to teachers in his monograph on creativity. According to Kagan (1968) a democratic classroom is a creative invention of its architects, teachers as well as students. Because its inhabitants are busy, sharing, inquiring and discovering in an atmosphere of mutual support and concern, creative learning both intellectual and social is occurring.

In the routine type of classroom the child is perceived as an object for intellectual and social nourishment rather than a thinker. He is treated as a member of the group without reference to his unique and individual personality. He is perceived as an empty vessel to be filled with facts and bits of information and overburdened with material that requires his total concentration. In such a situation, there is a danger that he will lose his own awareness and response to life; he will try to hide his real self to avoid the punishment of being different; he will become insensitive to his own inclinations and feelings which characterise the genuine human existence. He will become alienated and detached from any kind of meaningful endeavour (Moustakas, 1967). Going to school will be charmless occupation for him. In the words of William Blake:

"But to go to a school
    on a summer morn,
Oh, it drives all joy away,
    Under the cruel eyes outworn,
the little ones spend their day,
    in sighing and dismay . . ."

The non-significant status of the child in this type of classroom and the imposed passivity on him are the most dangerous pitfalls in contemporary education. They encourage a 'do not take a chance' attitude which is destructive to creative power. It is not easy to find examples of teachers deliberately setting out to develop in learners, the ability to vary their approaches to life situation, making them freely imaginative.

Teacher and Creativity

One of the most powerful ways in which a culture encourages or discourages creative behaviour is the way by which teacher and parents encourage or discourage, reward or punish certain personality characteristics as they develop in children or the behaviour which manifest those characteristics (Torrance, 1965). It has been pointed out that what parents, teachers and society encourages and discourages seems to be more important than heritability (Dehlevi and Torrance, 1979).

Classroom climate is crucial to learning process. The learning on the part of the students depends to a large extent on the socio-emotional climate in the classroom. The interaction between the teacher and the pupils in particular creates the climate of freedom or restriction for the pupils in the classroom. Thus the teacher's behaviour sets the climate in the classroom and conditions the learning of the pupil to a large extent, with realisation of the importance of socio-emotional climate of the classroom generated by teacher-pupil interaction.

A creative teacher can be expected to arrange an environment which extends certain invitations to search and experiment, which he is willing to take in the classroom and promote more pupil's participation. Since the teacher himself is creative, it is expected that he accepts new and novel ideas on the part of his students. Thus a high creative teacher is expected to accept student ideas to a greater extent than a low creative teacher. Further, since a high creative teacher is expected to create opportunities for imagination and creative activities, the pupils are likely to be engrossed in their work and as such there may be less confusion in the classroom of high creative teachers than in the classroom of low creative teachers. Thus it may be broadly hypothesised that teacher's perception of the students has a substantial bearing on his classroom climate, either promoting or hindering the creative development of students.

Lefrancois (1972) has emphasised that when the teachers are rigid, rule bound and authoritarian, they stifle creativity in the students. They insist on an excessive conformity to arbitrary regulations, give high grades for neat, correct unimaginative solutions to problems executed and reported in exactly the prescribed manner and refuse to admire the groping behaviour of a child trying to proceed towards the unknown. Unfortunately, teachers have to work under various constraints like syllabus, examination system which put a great premium on child's memory and factual knowledge. It is, therefore, hardly surprising that teachers and educators rate the industriousness of their good students much higher than their independence. Qualities like independence, non-conformism and curiosity suffer on account of uninspiring teaching methods. Few teachers seem to be aware of the potential creativity of their students and few would still dare to encourage it.

Types of Schools and Creativity

It is important to note that scientists, industrialists, politicians, artists, writers, and medical researchers of the future are currently in our schools. Yet present educational practices typically fail to foster creative growth among them; they perhaps even stifle the imagination of our students. The schools have ignored and have almost been indifferent to the area of man's creative abilities.

As has rightly been pointed out by Toynbee (1951), "the character of a society's institutions, attitudes and ideals determines whether potential creativity can blossom in it or not. One of the most convenient places where this can be accomplished is within the four walls of a school". Considerable attention is, therefore, being directed today to the identification of factors in the educational environment which are important from the point of view of creativity development.

In India, various types of school are providing education under the different administrative management set-ups. A controversial debate has been going on whether school education provided by these schools is of the same standard. While no one would agree that the standards of education should be allowed to deviate widely from one type of institution to another, it is equally desirable to know as to which type of institution is providing a better environment for creativity development. Obviously for obtaining best results in quality, ". . . talent has to be located early and allowed to grow in the best atmosphere and under the best teachers". (Indian Education Commission, 1966). Whether such teachers or atmospheres characterise the different types of schools is, however, a matter of conjecture as little research evidence is available.

The present investigation is undertaken to elicit answers to the question; Do significant differences exist between pupils studying in the various types of schools on different dimensions of verbal and non verbal creativity?

Assumptions

The following assumptions can be made in this regard:

1. That abilities involved in being creative are universal and are normally distributed.
2. That creative abilities can be measured reliably by available instruments of assessment.
3. That classroom climate can be measured.
4. That teachers' perception of students reflects their attitude towards creative behaviour of the students and can be assessed.
5. That the socio-economic status of students determines to a large extent their home learning environment and that it can be objectively assessed.

Objectives of the Study

The present study has been designed to achieve the following objectives:

1. To find out and compare the XI graders of four types of schools, namely, Aided, Government, Kendriya and Public in respect of their:

(a) Verbal creativity as well as its components,
(b) Non-verbal creativity as well as its components, and
(c) Total creativity (Composite of verbal and non-verbal creativity).

2. To determine the compare the classroom learning environment of the above mentioned four types of schools.
3. To compare high and low creatives of the earlier mentioned four types of schools and the total sample in respect of each one of the sixteen components of classroom learning environment.
4. To find out the relationship between each one of the sixteen components of classroom learning environment on the one hand and verbal creativity (A and B), non-verbal creativity and total creativity of the XI graders separately for each one of the above four types of schools as well as their total sample on the other.
5. To examine the prediction effectiveness of the different components of classroom learning environment in respect of creativity.
6. To compare the teachers' perceptions of an ideal pupil in the four type of schools, namely Aided, Government, Kendriya and Public.
7. To identify the relationship between teachers' perception of an ideal pupil and total creativity in each one of the above-mentioned four types of schools.
8. To compare the students of the earlier mentioned four types of schools in respect of their socio-economic status.
9. To identify school type-wise and total sample-wise relationship between socio-economic status of the students and their creativity.

Definition of the Terms

Some of the important terms frequently used in this study are chosen to be defined as follows:

Creativity

Instead of giving a separate operational definition of creativity,

Torrance's process-oriented definition is considered appropriate and adequate enough to serve the purpose of this study and therefore is adopted for use. Torrance describes creativity as ". . . a process of becoming sensitive to problems, deficiencies, gaps in knowledge, missing elements, disharmonies and so on; identifying the difficulty; searching for solutions, making guesses, or formulating hypotheses about the deficiencies; testing and retesting these hypotheses and possibly modifying and retesting them; and finally communicating the results" (Torrance and Myers, 1970b).

Student Creativity

Student creativity is considered to be the creative ability of students represented by their scores on various factors of verbal and non-verbal creativity such as fluency, flexibility, originality and elaboration as measured by Mehdi's (1973) test of creative thinking.

Classroom Climate

The concept of climate is relatively new. It is a concept which describes the role of participants interacting within the sociological and psychological framework of an institution. Classroom occupy a pivotal role in moulding the lives of schools pupils. Classroom climate may be said to be compound and not a mixture, where various elements meet, which can not be separated. Classroom climate may be pictured as a personality sketch of a classroom. Just as the personality describes an individual, so the climate defines the essence of a classroom. It is said there are 3000 to 5000 trait of personality, so too there are several components which create climate in a class. Climate, being the result of interaction between diverse personalities, is a much more complex phenomenon.

In Getzels and Thelen's model 'Climate' develops as a result of the teacher's transactional style, that is, the way in which he or she balances role requirements and personality needs within the classroom

The Editor Carter V. Good in *Dictionary of Education* defines classroom environment as: "The sum total of all the physical, social, emotional and mental factors that contribute to the total teaching-learning situation; for example, heat, light, seating, individual differences among members of the group, teacher personality, teacher-pupil relationships etc."

The whole idea is that the classroom situation has been interpreted in different ways by different educationists. The terms like 'Classroom dynamics', 'Classroom climate', 'Classroom learning environment' and 'Classroom inter-personal relations' have carried by different educationists for understanding classroom situation.

The investigator has adopted the definition given by Forehand and Gilmer (1964). After restating the widely held premise that behaviour is a function of the interaction between personal characteristics and environmental variables, they define 'climate' as a set of organisational properties which may influence the behaviour of individuals in an organisation.

As such, when an individual visits a number of schools, he can note quickly how schools differ from each other in their "Feel". He may find that in one school the teachers and the principal are zestful and exude confidence in what they are doing whereas in the other the reverse is seen.

Study of the school class group is particularly important since next to the family, the school is one of the most focal socialising agencies. Classroom climate or learning environment includes the profile of class group properties that are measurable. These properties include interpersonal relationships among pupils, relationship between pupils and their teachers, . . . and finally pupils, perceptions of the structural characteristics of the class.

For the purpose of measuring classroom climate, learning environment inventory (LEI) by Anderson has been used by the investigator.

Types of Schools

By types of schools we mean different kinds of schools (Aided, Government, Kendriya and Public) managed by different managements.

(a) *Aided School:* A school of 10+2 system (popularly known as Aided Intermediate College) which is managed by private body and affiliated with U.P. Board, Allahabad for examination purposes.

(b) *Government School:* A school of 10+2 system (popularly

known as Government Inter College) which is run by Government of U.P and affiliated with U.P Board, Allahabad for purposes of examinations.

(c) *Kendriya Vidyalaya:* A school (also called Central School) which is run by Kendriya Vidyalaya Sangthan of Central Education Ministry and affiliated with Central Board of Secondary Education (CBSE) for examination purposes.

(d) *Public School:* An independent English medium residential school managed by private bodies and affiliated with CBSE or ICSE for examinations.

2

CREATIVITY: A Theoretical Orientation

In the preceding chapter the need and importance of the study was discussed in the light of the need for developing creativity among students. It was argued that it can be done in the classroom. It was also pointed out that purposeful efforts in this direction are conspicuously absent from the teaching-learning process in our classrooms.

In the present chapter an attempt has been made to bring out some of the important theoretical considerations relating to creativity and environment.

Concept

Creativity can be understood as a process by which an individual can bring a new thing or idea into existence. For an artist, creativity is a process in which a great part of his being is involved; for an educator, it is a process of thinking which can be either nurtured or inhibited during the process of teaching-learning. The industrialist recognises it as a condition for new productions which have an economic value; and for a historian, it is an attribute of a great man.

Creativity is visualised as a multivariate phenomenon. The different perspectives that have been adopted to study creativity functions indicate that we are confronted with a highly complex phenomenon. This is well reflected in the great diversity of definitions of the term "Creativity" and variety of meanings attached to it. For example, McPherson (1960) collected 26 different definitions of creativity and in an interesting experiment in the Fifth Utah Conference, Mednick (1964) could get 395 different meanings in response to a stimulus word "creativity".

No doubt creative imagination is manifold and interacting. There are infinite number of ways to be creative as there are infinite number of ways of being intelligent. Therefore an investigator who attempts to conduct research in this field faces difficulty in defining that mysterious, awesome and thoroughly ambiguous concept called creativity, to his own and to others' satisfaction.

It is true that if creativity is to be studied scientifically, it must be defined in a way that permits objective observation and measurement. But MacKinnon (1970) cautions against accepting any single definition of creativity as final. He comments:

> "Definitions of creativity range all the way from the notion that creativity is a simple problem solving ability to conceiving it as the full realisation and expression of all of an individual's unique potentialities. One would be ill advised to seek to choose from among the several meanings, the best single definition of creativity, since creativity properly carries all of these meanings and many more besides. Creativity is, indeed, a multifaceted phenomenon."

This multifacetedness of creativity has led researchers to a variety of approaches to the study of creativity resulting in various theories and diversity in points of view about creativity.

Creativity, being an elusive concept does not have any universally agreed upon definition. Traditionally, it is taken to be an ability to produce a work of thought or imagination along new or unconventional lines (Webster, 1965).

May (1959) clarified the concept of creativity: "Whenever we face the question of defining creativity, it is important to make the distinction between pseudo forms of creativity i.e. creativity as a superficial experience, as aestheticism on the one hand and actual creativity on the other. Actual creativity, I define as the process of bringing something new into birth. In actual creativity, we do not deal with hobbies, with do it yourself movements, holiday painting or other forms of filling up leisure time, particularly on the part of the indolent classes.

It is the expression of the normal man in the act of actualising himself not as the product of sickness but as the representation of the higher degree of emotional health" (May, 1959).

Broadly speaking the definitions of creativity may be condensed to fall in four categories (Rhodes, 1961): as (i) Creativity as a product of ideas, (ii) Creativity as a process, (iii) Creativity as related to personality and (iv) Creativity as press or environment.

A global view of the creativity literature reveals that creativity studies are centred around four major orientations:

(i) The nature and quality of creative *Product*.
(ii) An actual expression of creative act and the underlying *Process*.
(iii) The nature of creative *Person*.
(iv) The environmental factors that initiate and foster creativity i.e. *Environmental Press*.

A Product Approach

Various approaches have attributed more to the understanding and meaning of it than did its latin origin 'Creare'. 'Creare' is to create. For Websterians, to create means to originate, to bring into existence something new, a work of thought or imagination; and creativity means intellectual inventiveness (Webster, 1977). This definition emphasises the product aspect of creativity.

Flanagon (1963) also believes that creativity is shown by bringing something new into being. He emphasises on the newness and lack of previous existence of the idea or product.

Newness or uniqueness seems to be a prominent feature of the creative product. Bruner (1962) found newness, surprise and originality in creativity.

For Parnes (1976), creative behaviour is that ". . . which demonstrates both uniqueness and relevance in its product. The product may be unique and relevant to a group or organisation, to society as a whole or merely to the individual himself (Parnes, 1976).

A Process Approach

Many researchers have directed their research activities to the study of the creative process. They attempt to answer the questions such as — How does actual production of a new concept or idea occur?; What process take place or interact while new creative ideas are produced?; What stages take place in creative thinking? and precisely try to find out what actually happens in creative thinking.

Maslow (1967) believes that creative thinking and for that matter all learning and thinking involves pre-conscious rather than conscious processes. There are other thinkers also like Gordon (1961), Gowan (1972) and Torrance (1975) who attribute important role to emotional, non-rational factors in outstanding creative achievement.

As early as in 1931, Rossman studied more than 700 prolific inventors and proposed the following set of steps of the inventive process:

1. Need is felt.
2. Problem is formulated.
3. Information is surveyed.
4. Solutions are formulated.
5. Solutions are critically examined.
6. New Ideas are formulated.
7. New Ideas are tested and accepted.

Basic to these different descriptions of creative process are the classical steps suggested by John Dewey (1910) and Graham Wallas (1926). Wallas suggested the following four steps of creative thinking process.

1. Preparation : Collection of Information
2. Incubation : Unconscious Work
3. Illumination : Inspiration of solutions, ideas etc.
4. Verification : Evaluation and testing of solutions, ideas etc.

These steps do not necessarily follow the same sequence and usually there is overlapping of these steps. Dewey's steps are identical to these stages.

If one thinks of creativity as a process, one can avoid the problems associated with cultural differences. It also helps to think in terms of the abilities involved in the successful operation of the process or for the production of creative products. Qualities of the product will result from the process itself. Personality variables or environmental conditions that facilitate or hinder the creative functioning can also be described by the process definition. That is why, Torrance prefers the process-oriented definition of creativity. He defines creativity as:

"A process of becoming sensitive to problems, deficiencies, gaps in knowledge, missing elements, disharmonies and so on; identifying the difficulty; searching for solutions, making guesses or Formulating hypotheses about the deficiencies; testing and retesting these hypotheses and possibly modifying and retesting them; and finally communicating the results" (Torrance and Myers, 1970).

This definition includes all the steps of the creative thinking process suggested by Wallas (1926) and Rossman (1931) and characterises creativity as a natural human process motivated by strong human needs.

Personality Profile Approach

The most exhaustive studies of children's creativity are those of Weisberg and Springer (1961) and Torrance (1962a). Weisberg found highly creative children rated higher than less creative ones on strength of self-image, ease of early recall, humour, availability of oedipal anxiety and uneven ego development. Weisberg considered humor as one of the best discriminators between most divergent and least divergent people (Weisberg and Springer, 1961). Hudson also describes humor as a distinguished characteristic of creative people. He attributed 'Avoidance of humour' among convergers to their general tendency to compartmentalise experience.

Another important study is of Torrance. He summarised the evidence on 84 personality characteristics that have been demonstrated to correlate with creativeness of children (Torrance, 1962a). There are 30 or more characteristics which can be considered sufficiently valid. When this list was compared with one used by Maslow (1954) in describing 'Self-actualising people', it overlapped almost perfectly (Craig, 1966). In turn, Maslow's list of characteristics of the creative overlap considerably the list of characteristics used by many others to describe psychological health i.e. Roger's 'Fully functioning person' or Jung's 'Individuated person' or Fromm's 'Autonomous person' etc. From this observation, Maslow infers that a creative person is a self-actualising person who has got good psychological health (Maslow, 1972).

Cropley (1967) observes that highly creative individuals are characterised in the cognitive domain, by possession of wide categories, willingness to take risks, willingness to 'have a go' and by high levels of flexibility (Cropley, 1967a).

Recently, interest of the Indian researchers in the creative child has also been reflected in many investigations (Raina, 1968a; Parmesh, 1969; Pachaury, 1975; Nair and Babu, 1977). Pachaury (1975) investigated into the teachers' perceptions of creative pupils. The teachers were found to value curiousness, courageous in convictions and independence in thinking and judgement in creative children.

Nair and Babu of Kerala University in their factor analytical study of personality variables related to high and low creative thinkers found three factors which characterise the creative group. These were social adequacy feeling, school inadequacy feeling and personal inadequacy feeling (Nair and Babu, 1977).

Environmental Press Approach

The conceptualisation and assessment of human environment has been strongly emphasised in educational literature lately. It has become an important area of theoretical and methodological concern of researchers. A growing body of knowledge demonstrates that in general, situational variables account for the significant amount of behavioural variance.

As far as environmental correlates of creativity are concerned, 'We are perhaps more in dark about environmental conditions which facilitate creativity than we are about any other aspect of the problem. Beyond obvious conditions such as the need for ample time in which to work freely on problems of one's own choice, Little is known' (Taylor and Barron, 1963). Eventhough there is a general paucity of research and the existing expertise is insufficient to give an exact idea about the nature of general environmental conditions conducive to creative growth, many factors have been pointed out by a number of recent researchers.

Creative thinking process has been considered as bipolar in which there is an interaction between a person and the environment in which he exists.

In "Creativity and Culture" Stein (1953) develops a strong relationship between the two elements of the title. He takes what he calls a 'bipolar view' assuming that an interaction between individual and environment is crucial to creative endeavour. Chambers (1973) considers creativity as a multi-dimensional process of interaction between the organism and its environment that results in the emergence of a new and unique product. A similar view is expressed by Parloff. He assumes that creative performance is a function of a complex interaction among such factors as personality structure, environmental influences and cognitive capacities (Parloff, 1972).

Piaget (1962) thinks that every act of thinking implies a balance between one's assimilation of the outside world to one's needs and one's accommodation of oneself to demands of the outside world. When this balance is broken in favour of accommodation, the child imitates reality. When the balance is broken in favour of assimilation, the child enters the realm of symbolic play — the realm of creative imagination.

"Imaginative play", writes Piaget, "is a symbolic transposition which subjects things to the child's activity without rules or limitations" (Piaget, 1962).

There is general belief that creativity may not simply refer to hypothetical disposition but may be inherent in certain environments and that it can facilitate or obstruct the development of creativity. Thurstone (1952) was convinced that creativity can be encouraged or discouraged by environmental conditions. Theoretical arguments by Schachtel (1959) and Kubie (1965) and some experimental evidence indicates that creative behaviour can be developed by the environment being controlled in appropriate ways.

School culture is an important determinant of the creativity of students. The teacher plays a very important role in providing conducive climate for creative growth in the classroom. A 'Laissez Fair type', non-directive, relatively unstructured environment seems to be favourable for creative development (Drevdahl, 1964).

To feel free, to express one's ideas implies the provision of an emotional atmosphere which is safe to experiment with one's behaviour, safe enough even to make mistakes without risk of being punished. Safety and affection are ranked high in the hierarchy of human needs. "Individuals have ideas but they are reluctant to express them. They have to be provided with a psychologically secure and free environment, explicitly or implicitly" (Bowers, 1965).

Home and family environment has been persistently indicated as a major influence on creativity of the child. The conditions under which the child grows in the family are vital to the growth of his creativity (Haronian and Sugarman, 1967). Saran, in his study of personality traits of Nursery school children found that individual development of a child with regard to curiosity, creativity, constructiveness and practical competence largely depends upon the proper home environment (Saran, 1970). Similar conclusion is drawn in Getzels-Jackson study also.

The parents of the creative children are found giving more autonomy to their children (Dreyer, 1966). They are moderately affectionate, non-rejecting and highly encouraging intellectual independence (Datta and Parloff, 1967). Respect in the family for autonomy and non-conformity, a respect for child's individuality and ability, parental tolerance and self-control are some of the factors of home environment found to be related to creativity (MacKinnon, 1967; Crutchfield, 1963; Schaefer and Anastasi, 1970).

Some basic factors in home environment impinging on child's creativity are birth order and family size (MacKinnon, 1967; Cicrelli, 1967); Sibling relations, serious illness (McClelland, 1963; Oden, 1968); Child rearing practices, rewards and punishments, need of achievements in the family (Feld, 1967) and mother-father behaviour (Dyk and Witkins, 1965; Dawson, 1967).

This review of the studies on environmental correlates of creativity reveals that though the field is not intensively studied, certain important factors like democratic conditions in group work, freedom of expression and movement, lack of fear of failure and provision of psychological safety, non-punitive provisions, encouragement and motivation, playfulness, breaking the barriers of conformity, recognition to individuality, family environment, child rearing practices, parental treatment and family background play very important role in proper nurturance of creativity of an individual.

Assessment of Creativity

Another critical issue related to creativity is the problem of identifying the creative potential, various types of criteria to assess creativity are used by different investigators. Getzels and Madous (1969) summarised them under the following categories.

1. *Achievement* — Highly recognised achievements like a Nobel Prize or any other mark of outstanding accomplishment as an index of creativity (e.g. Ghiselin, 1952).
2. *Ratings* — Evaluation by peers, teachers, supervisors, experts

etc. (e.g. MacKinnon, 1964; Drevdahl, 1964).

3. *Intelligence* — Performance on intelligence tests, superior I.Q. as a criterion (e.g. Terman, 1925).
4. *Personality* — Evaluation of Personality characteristics in relation to *a priori* profile of creative personality (e.g. Cattell and Drevdahl, 1955).
5. *Creativity test scores* — Performance on the creativity tests such as those developed by Flanagan (1958), Buhl (1960), Guilford & Merrifield (1960), Mednick & Mednick (1964), Torrance (1966) and others.

Chauhan and Tiwari (1974) surveyed the various materials used for creativity testing and found that ink-blots observation and drawings are frequently used to assess creative ability of the children. Poems, sketches, essays and stories written with the help of pictures, creativity tests like word construction, plot titles, ink-blots, unusual uses, consequences, mosaic tests etc. are frequently used to assess creativity amongst adolescents and adults by various researchers.

Creativity Tests

With the belief that creativity and intelligence are two independent abilities and with the conviction that traditional intelligence measures are inadequate to assess the mental abilities in their totality, several researchers attempted to develop specific tests to measure creativity. Guilford's D.P. tests, emerged from his factor analytical studies (Guilford & Merrifield, 1960) and Torrance's tests of creative thinking (Torrance, 1966) are most prominent among them and are widely used in hundreds of investigations.

Some other prominent tests of creativity are the Wallach & Kogan's instruments of creativity testing. The Getzels & Jackson's Test of creative thinking, Battery of originality tests by Barron, Flanagan's test of Ingenious solutions to problems, Mednick Remote Association tests and Minnesota tests of creative thinking.

Quite a good number of tests of creativity have been developed in India during the seventies (Passi, 1972; Kaul, 1973; Majumdar, 1973; Mehdi, 1973; Chauhan and Tiwari, 1974; Ram Chandra char, 1975 & Kundley, 1977). Some other prominent test are Kerala University test of creative thinking and tests of scientific creativity by Grewal and Singh. Most of these tests are based on Guilford's conceptualisation of creative thinking or on the lines of Torrance's Test model. Many of them measure general creativity but some are developed to measure creativity in specific areas of content. For example Majumdar (1973) has developed the creativity test battery to measure scientific creativity for the Science Talent Search Scheme of National Council of Educational Research and Training, New Delhi; whereas, Kundley (1977) developed his creativity test in Marathi to assess literary creativity of the school children. Most of the creativity test in India are developed for the doctoral studies. Some of them are published and now are Commercially available e.g. Mehdi (1973), Chauhan & Tiwari (1974).

Passi (1972) developed a battery of creativity tests to measure verbal and non-verbal factors of creativity of higher secondary school students. The battery consists of six sub-tests (both verbal & non-verbal). The sub-tests are: (1) seeing problems, (2) unusual uses, (3) consequences, (4) the test of inquisitiveness, (5) the square puzzle test and (6) the blocks test of creativity. Fifteen different scores like fluency, flexibility, originality, persistency etc., can be derived from the test battery. The reliability quotients by different methods range between .68 and .97 for the six sub-tests and the factorial validity of the tests against factors viz. verbal creativity and non-verbal creativity ranged from .31 to .75. Percentile norm for all the six sub-tests are established.

Another widely used tests of creativity is that of Baqer Mehdi (1973). Mehdi developed his test battery following the pattern of TTCT. It consists of four verbal test viz. consequence, unusual uses, similarity and product improvement and three non-verbal test viz. picture completion and triangles and ellipses. The reliability quotients estimated by test-retest method are .959 and .946 and the validity quotients obtained against teacher ratings are .390 and .385 for verbal and non-verbal tests respectively. Percentile norms for grade VII and VIII are provided. The test battery can be administered over a wide age range of sample from middle school to graduate level.

A somewhat different approach to creativity test constructions is observed in Ramchandra Char's Creative Response Matrices (CRM) (Ramchandra Char, 1975). He developed four matrices. CRM1 and CRM2 contain visual Figural Stimuli of varying ambiguity and complexity. The subjects are required to write in blanks provided in a row against each figure as many title like descriptions as possible.

CRM3 contains letter duplets. Each duplet is to be converted into as many triplets of equal sum as possible in two minutes. The letters are to be selected from the given set of nine letters each of which has a definite numerical value assigned. CRM4 contains sets of five single digit numbers. Each set is to be used in combination with the four fundamental arithmetical operations in a given fashion as many times as possible in four minutes to get positive round numbers as end product every time.

The battery measures four factors i.e. fluency flexibility, originality and elaboration and yields composite creativity index (CCI) consisting of eight standard scores. Validity of the CCI against teacher ratings is estimated to be .33. Reliability quotient found by K-R method is .71 (N=230). Standard scores and percentile norms are tentatively established.

Indian tests of creativity are greatly influenced by models of Guilford and Torrance. Almost all of them are validated against either TTCT or Teacher ratings.

Torrance test of creative thinking is available with parallel forms to test both verbal and non-verbal creative ability. It is used very popularly in hundreds of researches, including many Indian studies, yielding highly reliable and valid results.

TTCT consists of four batteries of test activities; two verbal, Verbal Form A and its equivalent parallel Verbal Form B; and two figural, Figural Form A and its equivalent alternate Figural Form B. A direction manual and scoring guide accompanies each battery, describing in detail how each test is to be administered and scored. Both the Figural and Verbal forms can be used from kindergarten through graduate level and can be administered as a group test or an individual test.

The test battery yields three verbal scores (fluency, flexibility and originality) and four figural scores (Fluency, flexibility, originality and elaboration). A composite score for either of the abilities or total score also can be obtained.

3

REVIEW OF RELATED LITERATURE

The previous chapter was confined to a theoretical discussion of the nature of creativity. Different schools of thought and research findings on the phenomenon of creativity were also briefly considered. It was concluded that creativity is a multiphasic mental ability which is amenable to change through the manipulation of environmental conditions.

In the present chapter, an attempt has been made to review all such studies which provide a back-drop for understanding the present status of research pertaining to the different variables included in this study, and for the formulation of hypotheses.

The variables have been classified as background or demographic, environmental and organisational variables. Socio-economic status has been taken as a back ground variable. Classroom climate and Teachers' perception about ideal pupil are taken as environmental variables. Types of schools (management basis) have been categorised as organisational variable. We shall take up the organisational variable first.

Organisational Variable

Types of Schools

Effect of different kinds of schooling was subject of many investigations (Ezekeil, 1966; Rastogi, 1967; Chatterjee, 1970; Ogletree, 1971; Aaron et al., 1974). Ezekeil (1966) found democratic school administration fostering creativity and initiative in teachers and broadening understanding on the part of all concerned. Rastogi (1967) and Chatterjee (1970) both found students of well equipped and advantaged schools better on creativity tests than students of ill-equipped schools.

Ogletree (1971) found that the steiner (private) schools followed a less restrictive and less intellectual approach in which art, motor activity and active involvement take precedence over academic intellectual learnings. Steiner school pupils obtained significantly higher verbal and figural scores on the creativity tests than state school pupils.

Aaron et al. (1974) did not find any significant difference in creativity scores of students under rural and urban schooling.

Gupta (1978) conducted a study to compare the creativity of students, studying in government and private schools. The sample of the study consisted 700 students of class VII to XI, studying in the four higher secondary schools of the city of Jammu. The mean, S.D. and '*t*' values were computed to analyse data. The findings of the study were that the students of private schools scored significantly higher than the students of government schools in different dimensions of verbal and non-verbal creativity.

For comparing the scholastic achievement, Chhaya (1978) made a comparative study of the achievement of boys and girls in physics of the three types of schools namely, central schools, public schools affiliated to Central Board of Secondary Education (CBSE) and public schools affiliated to Council of Indian School Certificate Examination (ISCE) of Bombay, Delhi, Calcutta and Madras. The sample consisted of 1200 students of classes VIII and X selected randomly from all the schools belonging to the three systems. The '*t*' test was employed to study the differences between different groups.

The major findings of the study were: (i) There was no significant difference between the mean achievement in physics of the pupils of classes VIII as well as X belonging to central school and the public schools affiliated to the CBSE. (2) The mean achievement in physics of pupils of the classes VIII as well as X of central schools was more than that of the pupils of schools affiliated to the Council of ISCE. The difference between the two was significant at 0.01 level. (3) The mean achievement in physics of pupils of classes VIII as well as X of the public schools affiliated to CBSE was significantly more than that of the schools affiliated to the council of ISCE.

Sultana Ahmed (1980) studied the different types of schools, viz., extremely advantaged schools, slightly advantaged schools, average schools, slightly disadvantaged schools and extremely disadvantaged schools in relation to creativity studying in classes VII, IX and XI, using Baqer Mehdi's Tests of Creativity. The school category was made in view of adequacy of Building, Library, Furniture,

Teacher-Taught ratio, Sports etc. It was found that the extremely advantaged schools pupils scored higher mean score on creativity.

Kusum Sharma (1982) designed her study to explore the relationship of creativity with certain background, psychological and organisational factors among students of 9th grade of higher secondary schools of Delhi. The sample consisted of 481 students (230 boys and 251 girls) from twenty different Government, Private aided, Public and Central Schools of Delhi. Data were collected through tests and inventories and analysed using various univariate, bivariate and multivariate statistical techniques. On the basis of findings, it was concluded that creativity was significantly related to organisational variable like management of school.

From the review of research, it is apparent that no study is available which has tried to compare the different types of schools in creativity and its dimensions in India, especially in western Uttar Pradesh.

In Uttar Pradesh, there are predominantly four types of schools operating — Aided, Government, Kendriya and Public. Types of schools on the basis of kinds of managements, exert a great influence on the persons studying in them as the prevailing atmosphere is different in all these schools.

Public schools attract the most affluent crowd and the staff members behave in a different way from that in others as they basically have a feeling of insecurity. In government schools teachers feel more secure and the students hail mainly from middle and lower class families. Aided schools strive for public recognition. In Kendriya schools, the students come from a more uniform background, hence the general atmosphere in these schools differs considerably.

Since the variable has not been studied in relation to creativity in Indian context at all. It was deemed desirable to study it in the present investigation.

Environmental Variable

Classroom Climate

In the past decade, the study of environment has emerged as an area of strong interest in social science research. This research has focused on the context, ecology or milieu of behaviour, particularly the social-psychological aspects.

Bloom (1964) made a strong case for environmental research in Education. Reviewing and summarising work on growth rates and environmental effects, he pointed to the development of measures of environment as crucial for accurate prediction and effective manipulation of learning. Studies by Pace and Stern (1958) and others on college environments and also by Dave (1963) and Wolf (1963) on home environments have shown powerful effects of contextual variables on learning (Bloom, 1964).

The school climate is very important to the growth and development of the creative abilities in a child. Obviously, a child spends a considerable portion of his most formative years in an environment which is radically different from his home environment and this leaves an everlasting impact on him. Among the environmental factors affecting creative abilities climate of the class is very important, published research on school climate and creativity is scanty.

It has been found that the conditions within the class are largely responsible for the classroom climate (Connor, 1960). The classroom with good climate was found by Connor to have more warm and friendly interaction, better teacher-pupil rapport, more opportunities for free self-expression, relaxed confiding students, more interest and enjoyment for the students. Freedom of expression and recognition of student ideas are the additions made by Enochs to this enumeration (Enochs, 1965). He found that the classroom in which pupils can express ideas, ask questions and have their ideas accepted, classified or in some way recognised by the teacher, is a classroom which promotes original ideas.

In his studies of social climates in ten high schools, Coleman (1961) found in the social climate evidences of forces that inhibit and facilitate various kinds of achievements among pupils. He suggests that changes be made in the reward structure of high schools to shift from interpersonal competition to intergroup competition in which group rewards reinforce achievement.

The work of Drews (1961) has also revealed a number of interesting clues concerning the forces that impede and facilitate creative growth. Her studies indicated that homogeneous grouping can be a far more facilitating factor in creative growth than is popularly thought.

Walker (1967), in comparison with traditional schools, found that high creative schools have psychological environments characterised by high aspirations level, high intellectual climate, high student dignity, high academic climate, low academic achievement, low group life, low academic organisations, low social form and low vocational climate.

Some studies reported that open classroom groups proved to be more creative (Torrance, 1964; Miruchin et al., 1969; Haddon and Lytton, 1971; Wilson, Stuckey and Langeyin, 1972; Harckham and Erger, 1972; Ruedi and West, 1973; Weiss, 1973; Tuckman et. al., 1973; Owem et al., 1974; Wright, 1974; NoGrady, 1975; Schnee, 1975; Mcportland and Epstein, 1975; Horwitz, 1978).

Torrance (1964) cited "rigid authority deprecates ideas offered by pupils". Including following types of environments in his study — Highly structured (Formal), Midroad I, Midroad II, Unstructured (Informal), Indeterminate (Anomie), he concluded that the most conducive environment to creativity was that characterised as "Midroad". Indeterminate environment gave lower creativity scores.

Febel (1966) found that student teachers in an 'open climate' school perceive the efficiency of the student teaching situation more favourable than student teachers in a 'closed climate' school. Haddon and Lytton (1968) in a study to evaluate the effects of differing teaching approaches on divergent thinking abilities in Primary schools found that informal, progressive teaching would promote these abilities more than formal, more subject-centered teaching.

Walker (1969) designed a study to investigate selected aspects of teacher personality in differing high school environments with the hypothesis that in high creative secondary schools, as compared with traditional schools, teachers would be less stereopathic (i.e. less authoritarian) and more rational. The inventory of beliefs, a measure of stereopathy, was administered to teachers in schools classified by type of climate. The findings indicated that teachers in high creative schools tended to be less stereopathic, but not less rational. The teachers in these schools were found to be more adaptive, flexible, outgoing, permissive and nurturant. In the classroom teachers were more stimulating and original; students were more initiating.

Haddon and Lytton (1971) in an attempt to verify the differential effect of differing school climates on divergent thinking abilities found that children in informal primary schools scored higher on tests of divergent thinking than in formal schools.

Marburg (1970) studied the relationship between classroom

climate and creative performance among 5th grade elementary school children. Empirical and observational data were collected to determine the effect of open and coercive classroom climates upon the overall performance and rate of gain of students on the Torrance Tests of Creative Thinking (TTCT). Two types of classroom climates were investigated: open and coercive. These were operationally differentiated on the basis of scores which the participating classroom teaching received on the Minnesota Teacher Attitude Inventory (MTAI). The classroom climates of the five highest scoring teachers were designated open; the classroom climates of the five lowest scoring teachers were designated coercive.

The investigator postulated that students in open classroom climates would have significantly higher overall performance scores and higher rate of gain than students in coercive classroom climates on the TTCT, but the data of the study did not support these hypotheses.

Ramey and Piper (1974) concluded that open children were superior to control in figural creativity but the controls were higher on verbal tests. Contradictory results were found by Abelson et al. (1974) who did not find any difference in the two groups on non-verbal creativity but the open groups showed a superior verbal level.

Indian Context

In Indian context very few studies are held in regard to classroom climates and creativity. Using analysis of variance technique Raina (1969) studied the role of school environment on creativity and found that students from the schools where creativity, originality and productivity were encouraged showed significantly higher performance on creativity protocols than students from the other schools.

In a study of creativity and school climate, Goyal (1973) found favourable results regarding the effect of school environment on creativity development. Three hundred students of grades VI, VII and VIII studying in three high/higher secondary schools, one judged to be 'High Creative', the other as 'Average Creative' and the third one as 'Low Creative' of Patiala district in Punjab formed the sample of the study. The criteria for selection were essentially those characteristics which Anderson (1962), Hallman (1963) and

Torrance (1963) used to describe as the 'Open System' of education and 'Responsive Environment' for it.

Three verbal creativity tests developed by the investigator on the lines of Torrance creativity tests were administered to the students in each school. The findings indicate that the more the 'Open System' of education and the more the 'Responsive' and 'Stimulating' environment in a school, the more the evidence of the development of creativity.

Similar results were also observed by Sharma (1968), who found that schools having 'open' and 'autonomous' climate had a significantly high achievement index as compared with closed climate schools.

Gupta (1974) in a research project entitled "A study of institutional climate and classroom teaching behaviour in relation to creativity", using Hindi version and adaptation of Joshi's Intellectual climate Inventory (renamed as Institutional Climate Inventory) on IX grade Science students of schools of Jammu city found that Institutional climate and verbal and non-verbal creativity were significantly related, though the extent of relationship was low.

Pillay (1975) found that schools with open climate differ in their capacity to introduce innovations as compared to closed type of schools.

From a review of the above studies, we can safely conclude that there appears to be a strong relationship between the classroom climate and creativity. Creativity in the classroom is not some thing that will just happen. Research indicates that conditions for creative thinking, the environment must be established (DeRoche, 1968). The open type or democratic climate is likely to be conducive for creativity development. The importance of conducive school environment can be had from Margaret's (1972) statement, "A gifted child may regress from original creative tendencies as he matures because of stultifying school atmosphere; from the once spirited child, he is transformed over night into a bored adult".

From the above studies, it is apparent that none has tried to relate psycho-social climate/learning environment of classroom with creativity especially in India. Further investigations are required before anything definite could be said on the relationship of classroom climate/learning environment and creativity in Indian context. Hence, it was considered necessary to find out the relation between the two variables.

Teacher Perception

One of the powerful ways of ascertaining whether a culture encourages or discourages creative behaviour is the way by which teachers and parents encourage or discourage, reward or punish certain personality characteristics as they develop in children or the behaviours which manifest those characteristics (Torrance, 1965).

Using his 'Ideal Pupil Checklist' Torrance (1965) studied teachers and other educators from five countries, the United States, Germany, India, Greece and Philippines. The United States sample consisted of 264 educators in the Buffalo, New York area. The German sample consisted of 94 elementary and secondary teachers in Berlin, the sample from India consisted of 375 elementary and secondary school teachers in Baroda area, the Greek sample consisted of 94 teachers in the area around the city of Volos, and the Philippines sample consisted of 147 teachers in training centres.

By examining the following list of the most valued characteristics of each group (country) we can very well know about the preferences of the teachers about the behaviours of students which they like most.

TABLE 3.1: Ten Characteristics Liked Most in Various Countries

	United States	Germany	India	Greece	Philippines
1.	Independent in thinking	Sincere	Curious	Energetic	Industrious
2.	Curious	Sense of humour	Obedient	Strive for distant goals	Obedient
3.	Sense of humour	Industrious	Does work on time	Thorough	Courteous
4.	Considerate of others	Independent in thinking	Courteous	Sincere	Healthy
5.	Industrious	Attempts Difficult task	Healthy	Non-conforming	Considerate of others
6.	Receptive to other's ideas	Independent in judgement	Self-confident	Remembers well	Does work on time
7.	Determination	Curious	A self-starter	Healthy	Self-confident
8.	Self-Starter	Self-confident	Industrious	Altruistic	Remembers well
9.	Sincere	Healthy	Affectionate	Self-confident	Willing to accept judgement of authorities
10.	Thorough	Adventurous	Determination	Courteous	Affectionate

Co-efficients of correlation were computed between the composite rankings of each country with the expert sorts of the creative personality, which are shown in Table 3.2.

TABLE 3.2: Co-efficients of Correlation between Composite Group Rating of Five Different Countries with Composite Q-sort Rating of Experts on Creative Personality

Countries	Number of Teachers	Co-efficients of Correlation
Buffalo, N.Y., United States	264	.51
Berlin, Germany	93	.47
Baroda, India	375	.35
Volos, Greece	94	.32
Manila, Philippines	147	.30

All the Co-efficients of Correlation are low indicating that according to expert judgement, the teachers of all five countries like characteristics which are inimical to creative development and behaviour.

Concluding the results, Torrance observed that teachers of all five countries may be unduly punishing the good guesser, the child who is courageous in his convictions, the emotionally sensitive individual, the intuitive thinker, the individual who regresses occasionally and plays or acts child like and the visionary individual. On the other hand, all of them may be giving unduly great rewards for being courteous, doing work on time, being obedient, being popular and well liked and being willing to accept the judgement of authorities.

Three studies in India (Phatak, 1964; Raina, 1970; Raina and Raina, 1971) on teachers', prospective science teachers' and teacher educators' perceptions of the ideal pupil have been made. All three studies made use of Torrance's Ideal Pupil Check-list. Phatak's study showed that the essential qualities of an ideal pupil according to her subjects should be: curious, does work on time, obedient, a self-starter, self-confident, healthy and courteous. The Baroda teachers of her study considered the following traits as punishable: disturbs class organisation, stubborn, fault-finding, talkative, spirited in disagreement, regresses occasionally and negativistic.

Raina's study using 40 prospective science teachers showed that they eulogised traits like curiosity, obedience, working on time, remembering well, self-confident, healthy, adventurous and courteous.

Raina and Raina (1971) designed a study to determine what concepts teacher-educators in India have of the ideal student in terms of what characteristics they believe should be encouraged or discouraged and compared the results with the concepts of teachers in the United States. When the 62 characteristics of the check list were ranked, a rank order coefficient of correlation of .76 was obtained between the rank assigned by the Rajasthan teacher educators and the United States teachers. It was also concluded that Rajasthan subjects emphasised the receptive nature of man and de-emphasised man's self-acting nature more than United States teachers.

Torrance (1967) in a study of the Ideal Pupil as judged by 21 Delhi teachers found a correlation of .86 between the rankings of this sample and a sample of 375 teachers in the Baroda area. The results of the present study on the perception regarding the ideal pupil indicate that teachers in these schools placed great emphasis on obedience, remembering well, affection, industriousness and sincerity. Compared with the teachers in most of the other countries surveyed, these teachers gave relatively low ratings to independence in thinking and judgement, being a self-starter, and willingness to take risks.

When the rankings of the Delhi teachers were correlated with those of the expert panel, a co-efficient of .11 was obtained. The findings indicated that there was little relationship between what the Delhi teachers considered an ideal pupil and what experts on creative personality regarded as ideal for creative development.

Since teacher attitudes and values seem to be of considerable significance in the emergence and development of creative thinking, a study of the qualities that teachers like to encourage and conversely condemn and discourage in their children was held up by Torrance in 1977. The 'Ideal Pupil Checklist' was administered to 67 teachers in all of the seven schools of Delhi. The schools were classified into three categories.

Category I : The traditional schools,
Category II : The national schools, and
Category III : The progressive christian schools.

The rank order co-efficient of correlation between the ranks assigned to 62 characteristics by the teachers in three categories of schools was worked out. The results are presented in Table 3.3.

TABLE 3.3: Co-efficient of Correlation between Ranking of Perceptions of Teachers in Three Categories of Schools

School Category	Category I School	Category II School	Category III School
Category I School	—	.85	.80
Category II School	.85	—	.69
Category III School	.80	.69	—

Results in Table 3.3 clearly indicate a high degree of association in the perceptions of three categories of schools. All the correlations are above 0.69. This significantly high degree of agreement suggests that all the three categories of schools agree to a very great extent on the type of qualities which they would like to encourage or discourage.

Comparison of the Perceptions of Teachers and Creativity Experts

"We obtain better index of the extent to which the values of each culture conform to creative values as measured by the experts sorts of the creative personality" (Torrance, 1963).

Therefore, a study in 1977 for the comparison of the teacher perception with the expert perception was made by Torrance. Table 3.4 presents the rank order of the 10 most desired traits and 10 least desired traits as viewed by the Indian teachers and experts on the creative personality.

The results in the above Table 3.4 indicate that the teachers and experts on creative personality view the ideal child in quite different ways. The results of the rank order coefficient of correlation between the two groups are shown in Table 3.5.

The correlations between the rankings of the Experts and Teachers are extremely low. The results presented herein concerning the Teachers' perceptions of the ideal pupil to the criterion (evaluation against expert nomination) show that teachers may be unduly punishing originality, individuality and spontaneity.

Similar results have been reported by Sharma and Raina (1980) and Raina (1982).

Since no study is available which might have attempted to know the perceptions of the teachers about Ideal Pupil in different types of schools of U.P., it was deemed desirable to study the ideal pupil perceptions of the teachers of different types of schools of western U.P. and its relationship with the creative performance of students of these schools.

TABLE 3.4: The Most Valued and Least Valued Traits of the Ideal Pupil as perceived by the Indian Teachers (1977) and Experts on Creative Personality

	Most Valued		Least Valued	
	Teachers Perceptions	Experts on Creative Personality	Teachers Perceptions	Experts on Creative Personality
1.	Does work on time	Courageous in convictions	Negativistic	Conformity
2.	Adventurous	Curious	Persistent	Willingness to accept judgement of authorities
3.	Courteous, Polite, Healthy	Independent in thinking	Talkative, Disturbs, Bashful	Fearfulness
4.	Obedient	Independent in judgement	Timid, non-conforming	Timidity
5.	Self-confident	Willing to take risks	Critical to others	Obedience
6.	Determination Industriousness	Intuitiveness	Fault-finding	Courtesy
7.	Curious, Inquiring, Independent in thinking, Remembers well	Become preoccupied with tasks	Haughty and Self-satisfied	Promptness in doing work
8.	Courageous in convictions, sincere	Persistence	Emotionally Sensitive	Socially well adjusted
9.	Affectionate, Loving	Unwilling to accept any thing on mere say so	Spirited in disagreement	Haughty
10.	Altruistic	Visionary	Emotional	Neatness and Orderliness

Background Variable

Socio-economic Status (SES)

Social class differences in creativity have also been explored in a number of studies but the evidence arrived at has not been unequivocal. Arguments have been given to justify the incidence of creativity amongst low as well as high socio-economic background. As Rogers (1968) points out: ". . . from early studies a perceptive picture has been drown of the personality characteristics that children of the slums develop to meet the challenges in their world. Several researchers have agreed that disadvantaged urban children are more spontaneous in their behaviour and actions, less conforming, more independent of their parents and more highly developed in motor skill than subjects from advantaged families. Any educator familiar with current research in creativity will recognise this pattern of a creative child".

TABLE 3.5: Correlation between the Ranking of Teachers from Three Categories of Schools (1977) and Experts on Creative Personality

Teachers	Experts on Creative Personality
Category I	.14
Category II	.12
Category III	.22
Total Group	.17

To elaborate, a child in a disadvantaged family observes from his earliest childhood how his parents attempt to put their very limited resources to multiple uses in order to get along to survive. He, thus learns to improvise, to substitute and to perceive the same object in varied ways and thus exercises his creative potential. The middle and especially the upper class child on the other hand has material resources in plenty to satisfy his needs and he is not required to improvise.

Secondly the child from low SES background is generally left on his own to a greater extent and is permitted to freely move around, explore and form his own ideas. Though this latitude on the part of the parents is incidental and not deliberate, it certainly has a liberating influence on the child which is likely to enhance his creativity (MacKinnon, 1962).

The schools catering to the disadvantaged are known to be least demanding since the teachers in these schools start with the mistaken assumption that these children do not have the potential to learn so that there is no sense in burdening them (Riesman, 1976). Thus, though these schools do not provide the necessary challenge and stimulation for their creativity to emerge, they do not overburden their mind with school work or knowledge where as a middle class and even more the upper middle class child, has little time left to call his own. With a relatively less burdened mind perhaps, the lower class child has been found to indulge in fantasy much more than the children from higher social strata (Feely, 1972). This is again conducive to the development of creativity.

Torrance (1978, 1979) states emphatically that the life experience of children from low SES prepares them for creative achievement. He argues that children who live in poverty and experience related disadvantages have to struggle for survival and this struggle poses a constant challenge to their creative potential so that they are likely to develop these abilities to an even higher degree than their more advantaged and affluent peers.

A study undertaken by Skager et al. (1960) with the purpose to determine whether the quality and quantity measures of accomplishments showed a differential pattern of correlation with scholastic aptitude and socio-economic status. The measures of SES did not relate to either of the measures of creativity. They concluded on the basis of their data that Income, position and even education of parents are less relevant to creative accomplishment of children. Dent (1971) also found that SES did not have any bearing on creativity.

On the contrary, in affluent families, exposure to variety of material concomitant with opportunities for learning in varied fields is likely to have a positive bearing on the creativity score of the students. Baughman and Dahlstron (1968), in a study of the relationship between children's family and their intellectual performance, demonstrated that the intellectual proficiency of a child was, in general, positively correlated with the socio-economic status of his family.

Nuttell (1971) also found that teacher rated creativity was positively related to socio-economic measures. McDaniel (1974) indicated that subjects from higher SES performed better on creativity than those from lower SES.

In India Raina (1968), Vohra (1975), Gupta (1976), Singh (1977), Rawat and Agarwal (1977), Thorat (1977), Singh (1978), Srivastava (1978), Awasthy (1979), Badri Nath and Satyanarayan (1979), Bhargava (1979), Jarial (1979, 1981), Sharma (1979, 1980), Ahmed (1980), Sharma and Jarial (1980), Singh (1980) and Vijai Lakshmi (1980) studied creativity in relation to Socio-economic Status (SES).

A good percentage of these studies have reported that creatives come from high SES. In his Ph.D. thesis, Raina (1968), while studying the socio-economic status of creative and non-creative students of higher secondary schools, found that higher creative group come from parents who were comparatively better in education than the parents of the lower creative students.

Jarial (1979) designed his study to find out the differences in creativity among the students with different socio-economic status background. The sample of the study consisted of 200 students selected from IX and X classes of various higher secondary schools of the city of Indore. The data were collected with the help of: (i) the Passi's Test of Creativity (verbal form) and (ii) the Kuppuswamy's Socio-Economic Status Scale. The mean, S.d. and '*t*' values were computed to analyse the data. The findings of the study were: (i) Students of high socio-economic status scored significantly higher in creativity than the students of upper middle, lower middle and low socio-economic status, (ii) the students of upper middle socio-economic status scored significantly higher in creativity than the students of low socio-economic status, and (iii) the students of lower middle socio-economic status scored significantly higher than the students of low socio-economic status on creativity.

Vijai Lakshmi (1980) studied academic achievement and socio-economic status as predictors of creative Talent. The sample consisted of 425 pupils attending six secondary schools in the Trivandrum district. The tools used were Kerala University Test of creative thinking and socio-economic scale data sheet. A high creative and low creative groups were identified and critical ratios were calculated with regard to socio-economic status. The results indicated that high creatives were found to come from a high socio-economic stratum.

Few studies reported that creatives come from average SES (Raina, 1968 and Awasthy, 1979). On the other hand Das (1957), Lalitha (1957), Badrinath and Satya Narayan (1979), Seetha Ram and Vedanayagam (1979), Rawat and Agarwal (1977), Chadha and Sen (1981) and also Sharma and Jarial (1980) reported that there exists no significant difference in creativity of students coming from high, average and low SES.

Rawat and Agarwal (1977) concluded that amongst the boys, SES does not have any bearing on creativity. With respect to fluency component of creativity, Sharma and Jarial (1980) observed that the students of high SES were superior to those of low SES. They reported that the students of high and low SES did not differ significantly in verbal flexibility, originality and total creativity.

Chadha and Sen (1981) studied creativity as a function of socio-economic status among 12th grade school students. The sample consisted of 116 students of 12th grade from a reputed Delhi Administration school. The Torrance tests of creative thinking and Kulshrestha's socio-economic status scale were used to measure creativity and socio-economic status of students. The data were analysed by employing *t*-test. No significant relationship was found between creativity and socio-economic status.

Taking into consideration the diversity in findings about the relationship between socio-economic status (SES) and creativity, it was decided to explore the relationship between SES and creativity in the present investigation.

A Conceptual Scheme for the Present Study

From the brief review of creativity, classroom climate, Teacher's perception about ideal pupil and socio-economic status, we can formulate a model for implementing the creative behaviour amongst students in the school.

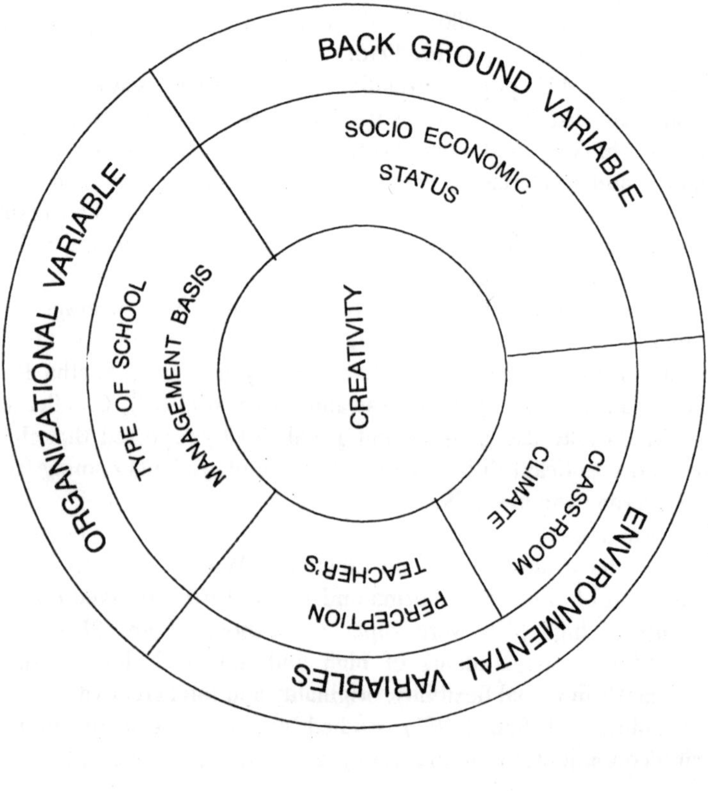

Taking all these factors into consideration, the present investigator proposes to investigate such a model which assumes that creativity of the students is a function of the joint effect of background, environmental and organisational variables. This model will act as a tool for optimum fostering of creativity by inculcating some or all of the factors.

4

METHOD AND PROCEDURE

This chapter deals with hypotheses, the sampling procedure, method of collecting data and statistical techniques used for treatment of data.

Hypotheses

The following hypotheses have been formulated for the study:

(1) The XI graders of the four types of schools, namely aided, Government, Kendriya and Public do not differ significantly in respect of their:

  (a) Verbal creativity as well as its components.
  (b) non-verbal creativity as well as its components.
  (c) total creativity (composite of verbal and non-verbal creativity.

(2) The classroom learning environment of the above-mentioned four types of schools do not differ significantly.
(3) High and low creatives of the earlier mentioned four types of schools and total sample do not differ significantly in respect of each one of the sixteen components of classroom learning environment.
(4) There does not exist any significant relationship between sixteen components of classroom learning environment on the one hand and verbal creativity (A and B), non-verbal creativity and total creativity of the XI graders of four types of schools namely, aided, government, Kendriya and public and the total sample on the other.
(5) Different components of classroom learning environment do not predict creativity in the above-mentioned four types of

schools and in the total sample.

(6) Teachers' perception of an ideal pupil in the earlier mentioned four types of schools do not differ significantly.

(7) There is no significant relationship between Teachers' perception and total creativity of XI graders in each one of the four types of schools.

(8) The students of the earlier mentioned four types of schools do not differ significantly in respect of the socio-economic status.

(9) Schools type-wise and total sample-wise relationship between socio-economic status of the students and their creativity is not significant.

Sampling Procedure

The sample for the study was selected in two stages. At the first instance, the selection of schools was made. Then the students and teachers were selected from the selected schools.

Selection of Schools

For selection of schools western region of U.P. was chosen. Varied kinds of schools exists in Uttar Pradesh. Only four types of schools of 10+2 system which are predominantly prevalent were chosen. These were private aided (popularly known as aided), government, Kendriya and public schools.

The sampling method used in this investigation was stratified purposive random sampling. The schools were stratified into four types of schools — Aided, Government, Kendriya and Public. The schools were randomly and purposively selected from each strata. Equal number of schools were chosen from each strata. Twelve schools were chosen, of which three were aided, three government, three Kendriya and three public.

Selection of Students

The population taken into consideration for the purpose of this study consisted of students of class XI from XII schools. One section of science students of class XI from each school was selected. In this manner 480 male students were selected.

Selection of Teachers

The teachers were selected from each school who were teaching from class VI to XII standard to assess their perception about ideal pupil. Total number of teachers selected were 275.

TABLE 4.1: Number of Students and Teachers in Different Types of Schools

Type of school	No. of students	No. of teachers
Aided	130	71
Government	140	68
Kendriya	112	73
Public	98	63
Total	480	275

Collection of Data

The questionnaires and inventories selected on the basis of feasibility of use in the study were administered on the students as well as teachers. For the purpose of collecting data, rapport was established with the students by giving self-introduction and the purpose and objectives of the study in brief. The subjects were assured the maintenance of confidentiality of their responses. The data were collected by administering the test in a group situation in one session of approximately three hours.

In case of teachers, the questionnaire was filled up individually as all the teachers were not available at one time.

There are three independent variables and one dependent variable. The dependent (criterion) variable creativity being sum of verbal and non-verbal creativity has seven components namely — fluency, flexibility, originality (of verbal test), elaboration-verbal, elaboration-non verbal, originality-verbal and originality-non-verbal (of non-verbal test).

Independent Variables

(i) Classroom learning environment
(ii) Teachers' perception about ideal pupil
(iii) Socio-economic status (SES)

Dependent (Criterion) Variable and its components

(i) Verbal Creativity (A)
1. Fluency
2. Flexibility
3. Originality

(ii) Verbal Creativity (B)
1. Fluency
2. Flexibility
3. Originality
4. Elaboration-Verbal] based on the performance
5. Originality-Verbal] on Non-verbal Test

(iii) Non-Verbal Creativity
1. Elaboration-Non verbal
2. Originality-Non verbal

(iv) Total Creativity (Composite of Verbal (B) and Non-Verbal Creativity).

Statistical Treatment of Data

Data thus collected were scored. The standard score shows the actual position of an individual just where he stands, with reference to the distribution of scores of a particular group. A comparative study of different groups can be made on the basis of standard scores because they can be directly compared with each other due to same positional meaning.

The Mean and Standard Deviation of raw scores of creativity, N = 480 were obtained as follows:

Fluency	$\bar{X} = 50.283$,	$\sigma = 12.623$
Flexibility	$\bar{X} = 33.373$,	$\sigma = 5.73$
Originality	$\bar{X} = 8.6$,	$\sigma = 5.89$
Elaboration-Non verbal	$\bar{X} = 42.910$,	$\sigma = 9.716$
Elaboration-Verbal	$\bar{X} = 41.637$,	$\sigma = 10.091$
Originality-Non verbal	$\bar{X} = 3.356$,	$\sigma = 3.797$
Originality-Verbal	$\bar{X} = 16.935$,	$\sigma = 6.744$

After calculating the Mean and Standard Deviation of raw scores (Garrett, 1958), the standard scores were calculated by the Strong's Method (1948). The formula used for calculating standard scores was:

$$S.S. = 10\frac{x-\bar{x}}{\sigma} + 50$$

where, $S.S.$ = Standard score
$\bar{x}$ = Mean of the raw scores
x = Raw score
σ = Standard deviation of the raw scores.

The data thus obtained were translated on data cards which were subjected to following methods of statistical analysis.

Univariate Analysis

(i) Mean and S.D. for all the variables under study were calculated.
(ii) *t*-test to see the significance of difference between any two groups.

Multivariate Analysis

Kendall (1957) pointed out that the variates are interdependent among themselves and hence we can not split one or more from the others and consider one by itself. Hence, variates must be considered simultaneously. According to Bock (1957), behavioural research typically involves problems in which several response variables are observed simultaneously which necessitates the use of multivariate analysis. It encompasses all the data from an investigation in one analysis. This approach results in a clearer and better organised account of the investigation. Techniques of multivariate analysis used in this investigation are as follows:

Step-wise Muitiple Regression Analysis

Step-wise multiple regression analysis is a method of analysing the collective and separate contributions of two or more independent variables; X to the variation of a dependent variable Y. The step-wise solution is a kind of multiple regression where in,

> "tests are performed at each stage to determine the contribution of each variable already in the equation, if it were to enter last. It is thus possible to discard a variable that was initially a good predictor" (Kerlinger and Pedhazur, 1973).

This method seeks the best set of predictors. Variables are added or dropped according to the statistical significance of their contribution to the prediction of criterion (dependent) variable. A step-wise procedure thus allows the data to tell their own story in terms of empirical first order interrelationship. Multiple correlations have also been computed for predictor variables in step-wise order. Beta weights, S.E. of Beta weights and *F*-ratios were also calculated.

The square of multiple correlation called the "Co-efficient of multiple determination" has been used for comparing the proportion of variance accounted for by different sets of variables. In this analysis by multiple regression technique, an attempt has been made to estimate the net effect of a set of predictors and also their joint effect. Method is referred to as the explained "Variance decomposition analysis" (Mukherjee, 1977).

5

DESCRIPTION OF TOOLS

To test the hypotheses mentioned in the previous chapter, a number of questionnaires and inventories were employed. The description of the instruments used for the survey is given in this chapter. Data were collected on the following tools.

1. Verbal Test of Creativity by Dr. Baqer Mehdi.
2. Non-verbal Test of Creativity by Dr. Baqer Mehdi.
3. Learning Environment Inventory (LEI) by Anderson, Walberg and others.
4. Ideal Pupil check-list by Dr. E. Paul. Torrance.
5. Socio-Economic Status Scale (SESS, Urban) by Dr. S.P. Kulshrestha.

Verbal Test of Creative Thinking

Recent advances in the area of creativity research have necessitated the development of suitable measuring tools and devices to assess reliably the creative potential of pupils for their proper education. Several attempts have been made to develop tests of creativity, especially in the United States. Torrance, Guilford and Wallach and Kogan have brought out their own batteries of creativity tests which are being extensively used not only in the United States but also in other countries including India either as such or with some minor adaptations.

All psychological tests whether verbal or non-verbal are culturally loaded and as such are not wholly applicable to a different culture. The need for developing tests which would be specifically relevant to a give culture is therefore obvious. The present battery is an attempt to meet this need by Dr. Baqer Mehdi.

The theoretical framework for the preparation of the test battery was provided by empirical studies on the nature of creativity.

Especially useful in clarifying the concept of creativity has been the distinction Guilford has made between two types of thinking abilities, namely, convergent thinking and divergent thinking. Guilford defines divergent thinking as a kind of mental operation in which we think in different directions, sometimes searching, sometimes seeking variety. The primary traits related to divergent thinking and therefore to creativity have been enumerated by Guilford as follows:

1. Sensitivity to problems
2. Fluency of thinking which has to do with fertility of ideas.
3. Flexibility of thinking consisting of two factors namely, spontaneous flexibility (defined as the ability or disposition to produce a great variety of ideas) and adaptive flexibility which facilitates the production of a most unusual type of solution.
4. Originality-indicated by unusualness of responses.
5. Redefinition, a factor which causes an ability to give up old interpretation of familiar objects.
6. Elaboration – an ability to construct more complex object.

In the preparation of the verbal and non-verbal tests of creativity, tasks pertaining to four of the above six traits viz. fluency, flexibility, originality and elaboration have been used. The four traits taken together give a fairly valid information about the creative potential of the individual.

Description of the Verbal Test

The verbal test which has been used in the study is a part of the total battery which consists of both verbal and non-verbal tests. The verbal test of creativity includes four sub-tests, namely, consequences test, unusual uses test, similarity test and product improvement test.

Consequences Test

The subject is required to think as many consequences of the situation as he can. The test encourages free play of imagination and originality. The time allowed for the three problems is four minutes each.

Unusual Uses Test

This test presents the subject with the names of three common objects – a piece of stone, a wooden stick and water – and requires him to write as many novel, interesting and unusual uses of these objects as he may think of. The time allowed for the three tasks is five minutes each.

New Relationships Test

This test presents the subject with three pairs of words apparently different tree and house, chair and ladder, air and water and requires him to think and write as many novel relationships as possible between the two objects of each pair. The time allowed for each pair of words is five minutes.

Product Improvement Test

In this test the subject is asked to think of a simple wooden toy of a horse and suggest addition of new things to it, to make it more interesting for the children to play. The time allowed is six minutes.

Rationale for the Activities included in the Test

In this section an attempt has been made to give a rationale for the selection of different types of activities included in the test.

Consequences

The basis of this activity is Guilford's Consequences Test or Torrance's Just Suppose Activity. The event is mentioned and the subject has to think of the consequences that may occur as a result of that stimulus, event, or happening, whether the happening is usual or unusual, logical or illogical. Thus the number of relevant responses produced by the subject yields a measure of his ideational fluency, the number of shifts in the thinking trends of the consequences gives the measure of verbal flexibility and the statistical infrequency of the response gives the measure of originality.

Unusual Uses

The basic idea of these tasks comes from Guilford's Brick Uses Test or Torrance's Tin Can Uses Test or Card Board Boxes Uses Test. Common things like water, wooden stick and a piece of stone are used as stimuli to let the subject's thinking go in different directions. The number of relevant responses may give the measure of one's ideational fluency, the number of thought categories the measure of verbal flexibility and uncommonness of responses a measure of his originality.

New Relationships

Mednick worked extensively with word associations and his definition of creativity is based upon remoteness of such associations. The items of this activity provide possibilities for scoring responses for fluency, flexibility and originality.

Product Improvement

This test of verbal imagination is similar to the one found in Torrance's Product Improvement Activity. Torrance used a picture of a Toy monkey, but in this test the subject is only asked to imagine a figure of Horse Toy. Apart from ideational fluency, the test also measures flexibility and originality.

Reliability of the Test

The test-retest reliabilities of the factor scores and the total creativity score were obtained on a sample of 31 students and are given below:

Fluency	Flexibility	Originality	Total Creativity Score
.945	.921	.896	.959

Validity of the Test

The validity coefficients for factor scores against the teacher-ratings are:

Fluency	Flexibility	Originality	Total Creativity Score
.40	.32	.34	.39

All correlations are significant beyond .01 level.

The validity co-efficients for factor scores and the total creativity scores are high enough (significant beyond .01 level) to place confidence in the use of the test.

Non-verbal Test of Creative Thinking

The test was constructed by Baqer Mehdi (1973). The theoretical framework for the preparation of the battery was provided by empirical studies on the nature of creativity.

In the preparation of the Verbal and Non-verbal tests of creativity, tasks pertaining to four traits viz. fluency, flexibility, originality and elaboration have been used. The four traits taken together give a fairly, valid information about the creative potential of the individual.

The non-verbal test which has been used is a part of the total battery which consists of both verbal and non-verbal tests. The non-verbal test of creative thinking is intended to measure the individual's ability to deal with figural content in a creative manner.

Description of the Non-verbal Test

Three types of activities are used for this purpose:

(i) Picture construction Activity
(ii) Incomplete Figures Activity
(iii) Triangles and Ellipses Activity.

(i) Picture Construction Activity

This activity presents the subject with two simple geometrical figures and requires him to construct an elaborate picture using each figure as an integral part. Emphasis is put on originality and elaboration. Originality is emphasised by the instruction that the subject should try to make as noval a picture as possible. The pictures are scored for elaboration and originality. The subject is also asked to give an interesting and unusual title to each picture. The titles may also be scored for verbal elaboration and originality, and the scores added to the verbal creativity score obtained on the verbal creativity test. Ten minutes are allowed to complete the task.

(ii) Incomplete Figures Activity

The activity consists of 10 line drawings which could be made into meaningful pictures of different objects. The subject is given 15 minutes for the 10 items. Each item is scored for elaboration and originality. Titles may be scored for verbal elaboration and originality and the scores added to the verbal creativity.

(iii) Triangles and Ellipses Activity

This activity has seven Triangles and seven Ellipses. The subject is required to construct different meaningful pictures in 10 minutes. Scoring is done for elaboration and originality. The titles are scored for verbal elaboration and originality and added to verbal creativity.

The emphasis is put on originality and elaboration. The total time required for administering the test is 40 minutes as 5 minutes extra are allowed after all the activities are completed.

The test-retest reliabilities of the factor scores and the total score were obtained on a sample of 50 students and are given below:

Elaboration	Originality	Total Creativity Score
.932	.947	.946

The Inter-scorer reliabilities using 34 test scripts were found to be .981, .980 and .917 for elaboration, originality and total creativity scores respectively.

Validity co-efficients for factor factor scores and the total creativity score against Teacher Ratings are as:

Elaboration	Originality	Total Creativity Score
.346	.329	.385

Correlation between the Verbal and Non-Verbal Tests of Creativity

The correlations between the verbal and non-verbal tests of creativity based on the total Creativity Scores were found to be .456 and .356 for the Urban and Rural samples respectively. It is recommended that both the tests should be used to have more complete information about the creativity of an individual. The test battery has been widely used by many researchers.

Learning Environment Inventory

Learning Environment Inventory (LEI) measures student perceptions of 15 dimensions of the social climate of school classrooms.

Classroom social climate or learning environment includes the profile of class group properties that are measurable and presumably have significance for research on classes as social groups. These properties include interpersonal relationships among pupils, relationships between pupils and their teachers and finally pupils' perceptions of the structural characteristics of the class. Representative dimensions of the interpersonal realm include cohesiveness and friction among classmates. Properties of teacher-pupil interaction include the extent to which pupils have formal rules to guide their behaviour, as well as the extent of democratic policy-making, disorganisation and teacher favouritism of some pupils over others. Pupils' perceptions of the speed of the class, the difficulty of the subject-matter and the amount of diversity in classroom activities relate to the subject and method of study. Among structural characteristics are included the acceptance of common goals toward which activities are directed, pupils' perceptions of their physical environment and the degree of stratification of the class into friendship cliques.

In selecting the 15 climate dimensions, an attempt was made to include as scales only concepts previously identified as good predictors of learning, concepts considered relevant to social psychological theory and research, concepts similar to those found useful in theory and research in education or concepts intuitively judged relevant to the social psychology of the classroom.

Description of LEI

The LEI contains a total of 105 statements (i.e. seven per scale) descriptive of school classes. The respondent expresses degree of agreement or disagreement with each statement on a four-point scale with response alternatives of Strongly Disagree, Disagree, Agree and Strongly Agree. Also the scoring direction (or polarity) is reversed for some items. It should be noted also that LEI scale scores cannot be summed to provide an overall score, as this would be contrary to the principle of multidimensional assessment. Table 5.1 lists the name of each scale and clarifies the meaning of scales by providing a description and sample item for each.

TABLE 5.1: Scale Description and Sample Item for each LEI Scale

Scale	Scale Description	Sample Item
Cohesiveness	Extent to which students, know, help and are friendly towards each other.	All students know each other very well. (+)
Diversity	Extent to which differences in students' interests exist and are provided for.	The class has students with many different interests. (+)
Formality	Extent to which behaviour within the class is guided by formal rules.	The class is rather informal and few rules are imposed. (-)
Speed	Extent to which class work is covered quickly.	Students do not have to hurry to finish their work. (-)
Material Environment	Availability of adequate books, equipment, space and lighting.	The books and equipment students need or want are easily available to them in the classroom. (+)
Friction	Amount of tension and quarrelling among students.	Certain students in the class are responsible for petty quarrels. (+)
Goal Direction	Degree of goal clarity in the class.	The class knows exactly what it has to get done. (+)
Favouritism	Extent to which the teacher treats certain students more favourably than others.	Every member of the class enjoys the same privileges. (-)

(Contd.)

TABLE 5.1 (*Contd.*)

Scale	Scale Description	Sample Item
Difficulty	Extent to which students find difficulty with the work of the class.	Students in the class tend to find the work hard to do. (+)
Apathy	Extent to which students feel no affinity with the class activities.	Members of the class do not care what the class does. (+)
Democracy	Extent to which students share equally in decision-making related to the class	Class decisions tend to be made by all the students. (+)
Cliqueness	Extent to which students refuse to mix with the rest of the class.	Certain students work only with their close friends. (+)
Satisfaction	Extent of enjoyment of class work.	There is considerable dissatisfaction with the work of the class. (-)
Disorganisation	Extent to which classroom activities are confusing and poorly organised.	The class is well organised and efficient. (-)
Competitiveness	Emphasis on students competing with each-other.	Students seldom compete with one-another. (-)

Items designated (+) are scored 1, 2, 3 and 4 respectively for the responses Strongly Disagree, Disagree, Agree and Strongly Agree. Items designated (-) are scored in the reverse way.

Reliability

The LEI can be used either to obtain scale scores for individuals within classes or to generate class means on each scale in order to estimate the climate profile of a class. Table 5.2 contains some preliminary information about each LEI scale's test-retest reliability (i.e. stability over time) and LEI Scale Means and Standard Deviations for individuals based on 1048 students.

The LEI is convenient and easy to administer. It does not mention the teacher at all and so does not pose the threat of other instruments that explicitly focus on teacher characteristics and behaviour. Moreover, in not singling out the teacher, the LEI acts on our assumption that the class members themselves, as well as the teacher, are an important determinant of the learning environment. Also it is possible to omit some scales that are not of interest in a particular evaluation. Over 200 American, British, Canadian, French, German, Swedish, Indian, Australian and New Zealand investigators have been encouraged to tailor the selection and adoption of scales to their specific research or evaluation objectives.

TABLE 5.2: LEI Scale Means, Standard Deviations and Test–Retest Reliabilities for Individuals

Scale	Mean N= 1048	Standard Deviation N= 1048	Test-Retest Reliability N= 139
1. Cohesiveness	17.71	3.14	0.52
2. Diversity	20.23	2.32	0.43
3. Formality	18.00	3.44	0.55
4. Speed	17.33	3.41	0.51
5. Material Environment	16.77	3.06	0.64
6. Friction	16.82	3.33	0.73
7. Goal Direction	17.96	3.80	0.65
8. Favouritism	14.18	3.81	0.64
9. Difficulty	18.72	2.80	0.46
10. Apathy	17.80	3.74	0.61
11. Democracy	17.53	3.16	0.69
12. Cliqueness	19.33	2.94	0.68
13. Satisfaction	16.77	3.65	0.71
14. Disorganisation	16.43	4.18	0.72
15. Competitiveness	17.04	3.33	0.73

Adaptation of LEI

The inventory was adapted to Indian conditions by the author by translating it into Hindi and adding one more scale i.e. sixteenth. Since the idea was to judge the class from creativity point of view, so a new scale Innovation was added in the inventory. For calculating reliability of the Hindi version and enlarged inventory, test-retest method was employed on 46 students of class XI.

The test-retest reliabilities of the sixteen scales of learning environment inventory are given below:

Cohesiveness	Diversity	Formality	Speed
.52	.41	.52	.53
Material Environment	Friction	Goal Direction	Favouritism
.61	.72	.63	.64
Difficulty	Apathy	Democracy	Cliqueness
.48	.61	.65	.67
Satisfaction	Disorganisation	Competitiveness	Innovation
.71	.65	.71	.49

Ideal Pupil Check-list

It has long been recognised that children tend to develop those characteristics that their teachers and parents encourage. In the domain of creative behaviour, what parents, teachers, and society encourage and discourage seems to be more important than heritability.

It we could determine what characteristics parents and teachers encourage and discourage, we would be able to understand and predict the behaviour of children under their guidance. Such information would provide useful clues for helping teachers modify their behaviour to facilitate creative growth among children.

Torrance worked for developing Ideal Pupil Checklist (at times called the Ideal Child Checklist or the Ideal Person Check list), an instrument which would provide a criterion of the productive, creative person. He made a survey of over 50 empirical studies which had attempted to differentiate the personality characteristics of some group of highly productive, creative people from a similar group of less creative people. The list, after several minor revisions, was finally developed into the 66-item Check-list. The instructions most commonly used are as follows:

What kind of person would you like the children you teach to become? Please describe the kind of person you would like for your pupils to become by using the check list of characteristics on this sheet. Check each of the characteristics that you think is generally desirable and should be encouraged. Then double check the characteristics you consider most important and should be encouraged above all others. Finally, draw a line through those characteristics you consider undesirable and should be discouraged or punished.

Wherein the 66 items are either checked, double checked, drawn through or unmarked, values are assigned as follows:

Double check	=	2 points
Check	=	1 point
Drawn through	=	–1
Unmarked	=	0

Reliability

Two tests of reliability were conducted with 43 students enrolled in the author's class in creative thinking at the University of Georgia. Near the beginning of the course, each of the 43 students was administered the Ideal Pupil Check-list and Q-sort formats. Near the end of the course (about 8 weeks later), the check-list was readministered in the check-list format. A co-efficient of correlation of .91 (significant at the one per cent level) as obtained between the pre and post-test rankings under the checklist format.

Validity

Content validity is assured through the procedures used in developing the check-list. The 66 items represent personality characteristics that have been found in empirical studies to differentiate productive, creative persons from persons who are less productive and creative.

The first tests of the validity of the Ideal Pupil check-list were based upon data obtained by R.E. Myers, Richard Dawson and the author in workshops with teachers. Where teachers responded to creative approaches and the atmosphere of the school seemed to promote creative behaviour, the rankings of the experts on the productive, creative person criterion were usually .50 or above. Where the teachers were unresponsive and the children seemed to be fettered, the correlations were quite low (below .30).

The first large-scale validation of the check-list came from a set of cross-cultural studies involving students and teachers from 10 diverse societies. The Torrance Tests of Creative Thinking (1966, 1974) were administered to 500 to 1100 children in grades one through six in each of the 10 samples and the teachers of these children were administered the Ideal Pupil check-list (Torrance, 1967). For each of the 10 groups a set of rankings was derived and these rankings were correlated with those of the expert panel. The mean standard scores for the figural and verbal creativity measures were obtained and summed. The results are show in Table 5.3:

TABLE 5.3: Ideal Pupil Check-list

Culture group	Creativity		Ideal Pupil	
	Index	Rank	Index	Rank
Minnesota, USA	97.2	1	.43	1
California, USA	96.2	2	.40	2
West Germany	92.5	3	.37	3
Chinese, Singapore	84.5	4	.28	5
Tamils, Singapore	82.44	5	.28	5
Western Australia	82.1	6	.19	8
Malays, Singapore	81.0	7	.28	5
Georgia Blacks, USA	80.0	8.5	.21	7
India, New Delhi	80.0	8.5	.11	10
Western Samoa	79.3	10	.17	9

When these two sets of rankings are correlated, a coefficient of .94 results. Thus, cultures assessed against the criterion of the ideal, productive, creative person seems to be related significantly to the level of creativity of the children being reared in those cultures.

Socio-economic Status Scale (SESS)

Socio-economic Status is an important social variable and hence the need for the study of socio-economic background of the individual, the appraisal of socio-economic stratum is of immense importance in any psychological study because one's position in the social hierarchy is correlated with attitudes, values, school achievement, emotional stability, and many other phenomena (Gough, 1948; Gordon 1952 and Kohn 1959).

In order to measure the socio-economic status of the students, the Socio-economic Status Scale prepared by Dr. S.P. Kulshrestha (1980) was used. The instrument contains 20 items covering such areas as

Parental occupation, Father's/Guardian's education, Monthly income, House type, House-hold material possessions, Cultural sub-factors, Education of siblings, Level of aspiration, Concept of social prestige and Belief in caste etc.

Test-Retest reliability of the scale is reported in the manual to be .87 (N= 100).

The opinions of five Sociologists, five Psychologists, five Economists and five Educationists were sought and they found the scale valid for the purpose. Thus scale possesses content and construct validity. The validity of the scale was also calculated by comparing the scale with Dr. Kuppuswamy's and Pandey's socio-economic status questionnaire. The co-efficient of correlations were found .57 and .89 respectively.

It is a simple scale and popularly used in educational research.

6

ANALYSIS OF DATA AND RESULTS

This chapter proposes to analyse, organise, and interpret the data and results that have been obtained consequent to application of the research strategy. The whole data have been organised and presented in the following pages under sections as below:

A. School administrative set-up and creativity
B. Classroom learning environment and creativity
C. Teachers' perception of ideal pupils and creativity
D. Socio-economic status and creativity.

In Section A, data and results have been presented and discussed to study the level and differences of creativity among students studying in four types of schools. Results, to study classroom learning environment of four types of schools and its relationship with creativity of students, are presented and discussed in Section B. The Section C, deals with the discussion of data and results to compare the teacher's perception of an ideal pupil in four types of schools and to see its relationship with creative performance of the students of these schools. In Section D, data and results are presented and discussed to study socio-economic status of the students of four types of schools and its relationship with creativity of the students. Further, it is proposed to interpret the data sectionwise and tablewise.

SECTION A

School Administrative Set-up and Creativity

In the present study four types of schools, namely Aided, Government, Kendriya and Public have been studied. Administratively two of them namely, Government and Kendriya are governed by government — the state and the central, whereas the two others namely, Aided and Public are governed by private enterprise. Since educational administrative set-up in all these schools differ, the influence of these differences in the educational administrative set-up on creativity was sought to be studied through the present research. It was hypothesised that there will not be significant differences in the creativity of an average student of the four types of schools' Aided, Government, Kendriya and Public. Tables 6.1 and 6.2 throw light on the efficacy of the hypothesis as well as on the extent of achievement of the first objective of the study, Interpretation of the data contained in the Tables 6.1 and 6.2 as stated earlier will follow their sequence of presentation.

Table 6.1 yields the information as below:

(i) Mean and Standard deviation scores of the XI graders studying in Aided, Government, Kendriya and Public schools pertaining to fluency, flexibility, originality, elaboration (verbal), originality (verbal), elaboration (non-verbal), originality (non-verbal), verbal creativity (A), verbal creativity (B), non-verbal creativity components of creativity as well as as total creativity.

(ii) By and large the mean scores of creativity components, mainly, fluency, flexibility, originality, elaboration (verbal), originality (verbal), elaboration (non-verbal), originality (non-verbal) are of approximately average level for students of all the four types of schools specified above. The mean scores ranges between 48.37 to 51.21 in the case of fluency component of creativity, 49.30 to 52.26 in the case of flexibility component, 47.64 to 52.07 for originality, 46.34 to 51.98 for elaboration (verbal), 46.57 to 55.14 for originality (verbal), 48.49 to 53.73 for elaboration (non-verbal) and 46.41 to 55.59 for originality (non-verbal). These scores need to be understood in the context of the fact that as per normal probability curve distribution characteristics, the range of T-scores is between 40 to 60 at the middle category of the curve, mainly average category. All the mean scores mentioned above are between 40 to 60, and therefore stated earlier are of average value.

(iii) In the context of above observations, it can be deduced that XI graders differentiated on the basis of their types of schools, do not differ markedly in respect of components of creativity.

TABLE 6.1: **Mean and S.D. Values of Creativity and its Dimensions in Four Types of Schools**

Creativity and its Components	Types of Schools							
	Aided		Government		Kendriya		Public	
	$\overline{X}$	σ	$\overline{X}$	σ	$\overline{X}$	σ	$\overline{X}$	σ
1. Fluency	50.20	10.74	50.07	9.98	51.21	8.40	48.37	10.38
2. Flexibility	49.55	10.06	49.21	10.72	52.26	8.78	49.30	10.04
3. Originality	47.64	8.82	51.18	10.39	52.07	11.35	48.78	8.68
4. Elaboration (Verbal)	46.34	7.54	49.79	11.05	51.38	10.13	51.98	10.08
5. Originality (Verbal)	46.57	8.87	48.93	7.84	51.08	10.71	55.14	10.92
6. Elaboration (Non-verbal)	48.55	8.83	48.49	9.21	53.73	10.57	49.79	10.39
7. Originality (Non-verbal)	46.41	6.82	47.44	8.32	52.31	11.55	55.59	11.00
8. Verbal Creativity (A)	147.39	26.46	150.46	26.62	155.54	24.41	146.44	26.35
9. Verbal Creativity (B)	240.30	34.34	249.18	37.84	257.99	36.32	253.56	39.49
10. Non-verbal Creativity	94.96	13.53	95.92	14.98	106.04	19.93	105.38	18.74
11. Total Creativity	335.26	43.49	345.10	46.89	364.04	49.81	358.94	50.59

(iv) Although XI graders as a group related to different schools show the development of various components of creativity up to average level, they show noticeable differences in variations on these very components. As for example students of Aided and Public schools show marked variations on fluency in comparison to Government and Kendriya.

(v) By and large, it seems students studying in Kendriya Vidyalayas are marginally superior to students studying in the remaining three types of schools on various components of creativity as well as total creativity.

(vi) Students studying in Aided and Government schools show appreciable similarity on the level of fluency, flexibility, elaboration (non-verbal), originality (non-verbal) and non-verbal creativity. They, however, shows marginal differences with relatively better performance of the students of Government schools on originality, elaboration (verbal) originality (verbal), verbal creativity (A and B) and total creativity.

(vii) By and large students of Public schools, surprisingly enough have been found to be less developed in fluency, flexibility and originality than students of Aided, Government and Kendriya schools. But on elaboration (verbal and non-verbal), verbal creativity (B), non-verbal creativity as well as total creativity, they have been found to be better to students of Aided and Government schools and to be better in originality (verbal and non-verbal) to students of Aided, Government and Kendriya schools.

(viii) From the observations enumerated above, it can be said that students who have been examined in the present study show similarity on some components of creativity and show dissimilarity in respect of some other creativity components.

The data contained in Table 6.1 throw light on the extent to which the first objective of the study has been achieved. It will be recalled that the current study was initiated with a view to ascertain the level of creativity and its components among XI graders studying in four types of schools — namely, Aided, Government, Kendriya and Public. By and large school-type-wise Mean and S.D. data for creativity and its components lead to the generalisation that the creativity level of each one of the four types of schools approaches an average level because the mean score for each type of the school ranges between

40 to 60 T scores. This generalisation is in contrast to the general belief that students studying in Public schools are more creative than such schools as are run through grants from government or administered by State and Central Government. Although it is true that students in Public schools are usually drawn from higher socio-economic strata of the society and students of the Aided schools belong to relatively less affluent section of the society and the general assumption is that students drawn from the former socio-economic status are more creative than those belonging to low socio-economic status. The observation made in the present study suggests that differences in socio-economic status are not necessarily related to differences in creativity. Earlier research conducted with a view to explore the relationship between socio-economic status and creativity bear out that relationship between socio-economic status and creativity is indeed of marginal value only. Since socio-economic status does not significantly influence creativity, therefore, it is only logical to observe the average students of a school not to show very significant differences in this regard from an average student studying in other schools. The results of the table, therefore, need to be appreciated in the context of findings drawn in earlier research studies.

While Table 6.1 indicates the level of creativity among students studying in Aided, Government, Kendriya and Public schools, the Table 6.2 indicates the influence of administrative set-up in these schools on the creativity of the students. This objective has been accomplished by subjecting the data to *F*- and *t* tests. The *F*- values obtained on total creativity, verbal and non-verbal creativity as well as on their components have been found to be significant for originality ($F=5.214^{**}$), elaboration verbal ($F=7.922^{**}$), originality verbal ($F=16.142^{**}$), elaboration non-verbal ($F=7.592^{**}$), originality non-verbal ($F=23.363^{**}$), verbal creativity (A) ($F=2.728^{*}$, verbal creativity (B) ($F=5.016^{**}$), non-verbal creativity ($F=14.852^{**}$) and total creativity ($F=9.007^{**}$). No significant F-value has been observed on fluency ($F=1.437$) and flexibility ($F=2.436$) components of creativity. The significance of *F*-value in respect of as many as seven of its components as well as in total creativity shows that there are significant differences in the creativity level of the XIth graders studying in the four types of schools. This observation also go to support the view expressed earlier that the school administrative set-up is a very important factor in the growth of creativity. This inference is also supported by the earlier findings drawn by Ezekeil (1966), Ogletree (1971), Gupta (1978), Sultana Ahmed (1980) and Sharma (1982). It also indicates that the null hypothesis proposed in this study does not get any support from the data and therefore, it is rejected. Table 6.2 besides revealing the efficacy of the hypothesis also contain *t*-values indicative of the significance of difference between XI graders of two schools at a time on various components of creativity as well as total creativity. The between group comparisons of the students have yielded the following facts.

Creativity among Students of Aided and Government Schools

Significant differences have been observed among students of above schools on originality (t=2.99**), elaboration verbal (t=2.97**), originality verbal (t=2.31*), verbal creativity B (t=2.01*) components of creativity. From Table 6.1, it is found that students of Government schools have higher mean scores on originality ($\bar{x}=51.18$), elaboration verbal ($\bar{x}=49.79$), originality verbal ($\bar{x}=48.93$) and verbal creativity B ($\bar{x}=249.18$) than students of Aided schools. This shows that students of Government schools have relatively more originality, elaboration verbal, originality verbal and verbal creativity than students of Aided schools.

Creativity among Students of Aided and Kendriya Schools

Significant differences have been observed among students of above schools on flexibility (t=2.17*), originality (t=3.40**), elaboration verbal (t=4.40**), originality verbal (t=3.57**), elaboration non-verbal (t=4.14**), originality non-verbal (t=4.90**), verbal creativity A (t=2.50*), verbal creativity B(t=3.87**), non-verbal creativity (t=5.10**) and total creativity (t=4.78**). From Table 6.1, it is found that students of Kendriya schools have higher mean scores on flexibility ($\bar{x}=52.26$), originality ($\bar{x}=52.07$), elaboration verbal ($\bar{x}=51.38$), originality verbal ($\bar{x}=51.08$), elaboration non-verbal ($\bar{x}=53.73$), originality non-verbal ($\bar{x}=52.31$), verbal creativity A ($\bar{x}=155.54$), verbal creativity B ($\bar{x}=257.99$), non-verbal creativity ($\bar{x}=106.04$), and total creativity ($\bar{x}=364.04$) than students of Aided schools. This shows that students of Kendriya schools with the exception of one component of creativity, namely fluency are superior to the students of Aided schools on creativity and its other dimensions.

TABLE 6.2: *F* and *t*-values of XI Graders on Creativity and Its Dimensions in Four Types of Schools

Difference on	Among Groups (F-value)	Between XI Graders of Schools (*t*-values)					
		A and G	A and K	A and P	G and K	G and P	K and P
1. Fluency	1.44	0.10	0.85	1.40	1.01	1.39	2.35*
2. Flexibility	2.44	0.27	2.17*	0.21	2.39*	0.04	2.25*
3. Originality	5.21**	2.99**	3.40**	0.97	0.65	1.87	2.33*
4. Elaboration (Verbal)	7.92**	2.97**	4.40**	4.81**	1.17	1.55	0.43
5. Originality (Verbal)	16.14**	2.31*	3.57**	6.51**	1.83	5.09**	2.70**
6. Elaboration (Non-verbal)	7.59**	0.06	4.14**	0.96	4.19**	1.01	2.71**
7. Originality (Non-verbal)	23.36**	1.10	4.90**	7.71**	3.88**	6.48**	2.09*
8. Verbal Creativity (A)	2.73*	0.94	2.50*	0.38	1.59	1.25	2.71**
9. Verbal Creativity (B)	5.02**	2.01*	3.87**	2.69**	1.86	0.86	0.84
10. Non-verbal Creativity	14.85**	0.55	5.10**	4.85**	4.58**	4.30**	0.25
11. Total Creativity	9.01**	1.78	4.78**	3.78**	3.09**	2.16*	0.73

A = Aided School; G = Government school; K = Kendriya school; P = Public school; * = Significant at 5 per cent level; ** = Significant at 1 per cent level

Creativity among Students of Aided and Public Schools

Significant differences have been observed among students of above schools on elaboration verbal (t=4.81**), originality verbal (t=6.51**), originality non-verbal (t=7.71**), verbal creativity B (t=2.69**), non-verbal creativity (t=4.85**) and total creativity (t=3.78**). From Table 6.1, it is found that students of Public schools have higher mean scores on elaboration verbal ($\bar{x}$=51.98), originality verbal ($\bar{x}$=55.14), originality non-verbal ($\bar{x}$=55.59), verbal creativity B ($\bar{x}$=253.56), non-verbal creativity ($\bar{x}$=105.38), and total creativity ($\bar{x}$=358.94) than students of Aided schools. This shows that students of Public schools are relatively superior to students of Aided schools on creativity as well as its components.

Creativity among Students of Government and Kendriya Schools

Significant differences have been observed among students of above schools on flexibility (t=2.39*), elaboration non-verbal (t=4.19**), originality non-verbal (t=3.88**), non-verbal creativity (t=4.58**) and total creativity (t=3.09**). From Table 6.1, it is found that students of Kendriya schools have higher mean scores on flexibility ($\bar{x}$=52.26), elaboration non-verbal ($\bar{x}$=53.73), originality non-verbal ($\bar{x}$=52.31), non-verbal creativity ($\bar{x}$=106.04) and total creativity ($\bar{x}$=364.04) than students of Government schools. This shows that students of Kendriya schools are relatively superior to students of Government schools on creativity as well as its components.

Creativity among Students of Government and Public Schools

Significant differences have been found among students of above schools on originality verbal (t=5.09**), originality non-verbal (t=6.48**), non-verbal creativity (t=4.30**) and total creativity (t=2.16*). From Table 6.1, it is found that students of Public schools have higher mean scores on originality verbal ($\bar{x}$=55.14), originality non-verbal ($\bar{x}$=55.59), non-verbal creativity ($\bar{x}$=105.38) and total creativity ($\bar{x}$=358.94) than students of Government schools. This shows that students of Public schools are relatively superior to students of Government schools on creativity as well as its components.

Creativity among Students of Kendriya and Public Schools

Significant differences have been found among students of above schools on fluency (t=2.35*), flexibility (t=2.25*), originality (t=2.33*), originality verbal (t=2.70**), elaboration non-verbal (t=2.71**), originality non-verbal (t=2.09*) and verbal creativity A (t=2.71**). From Table 6.1, it is found that students of Kendriya schools have higher mean scores on fluency ($\bar{x}$=51.21), flexibility ($\bar{x}$=52.26), originality ($\bar{x}$=52.07), elaboration non-verbal ($\bar{x}$=53.73) and verbal creativity A ($\bar{x}$=155.54) than students of Public schools with the exception of two components, namely, originality verbal ($\bar{x}$=55.14) and originality non-verbal ($\bar{x}$=55.59) in which Public schools have higher mean scores than Kendriya schools. This shows that students of Kendriya schools have relatively more fluency, flexibility, originality, elaboration non-verbal and verbal creativity (A) than students of Public school who show superiority over students of Kendriya schools in originality verbal and originality non-verbal.

The data interpreted above leads to the following generalisations:

1. Each type of school has a distinctive educational administrative set-up.
2. The learning environment of Kendriya Vidyalayas seems to be better to other types of schools.
3. Students studying in the four types of schools differ significantly in respect of their creativity as well as on most of its dimensions.
4. Creativity, has been found to be much highly developed in Kendriya Vidyalayas and much less in Aided schools.
5. There is a relationship between educational administrative set-up of a school and the growth of creativity and its components.

SECTION B

Classroom Learning Environment and Creativity

Earlier has explicitly brought out the fact that creativity unmasks itself in a conducive environment. As against, a school environment having opposite characteristics has fewer possibilities for identifying and nurturing creativity. It was assumed in this study that the learning environmental conditions in four types of schools namely, Aided, Government, Kendriya and Public will be different and therefore, the investigator proceeded to examine the assumption by proposing the second objective of the study. However, for purpose of keeping an unbiased attitude, it was hypothesised that differences in school type will not be related to differences in their learning environment. Table 6.3 furnishes data to indicate the extent to which the null hypothesis framed in this study is valid.

TABLE 6.3: Mean and S.D. Values of XI Graders of Four Types of Schools on Learning Environment Dimensions

Components of Learning Environment	Types of Schools							
	Aided		Government		Kendriya		Public	
	$\bar{x}$	σ	$\bar{x}$	σ	$\bar{x}$	σ	$\bar{x}$	σ
Cohesiveness	19.19	3.49	18.84	3.57	20.68	3.06	20.37	3.35
Diversity	20.05	2.56	20.00	2.55	20.73	2.31	20.03	1.89
Formality	20.68	3.56	21.04	4.07	18.71	3.22	18.44	2.00
Speed	19.43	2.70	18.93	2.35	17.72	2.53	17.11	2.61
M. Environment	18.79	4.38	17.44	3.64	20.21	2.81	18.87	3.64
Friction	18.55	3.33	19.09	4.07	19.18	3.27	18.08	3.29
Goal-Direction	20.82	3.50	20.25	3.24	20.72	3.08	19.02	3.31
Favouritism	17.18	4.26	17.44	4.75	17.83	4.02	17.02	3.94
Difficulty	17.18	2.34	17.43	2.62	17.35	2.46	18.53	2.48
Apathy	14.68	3.64	15.04	4.19	14.99	4.01	16.92	3.74
Democracy	16.74	3.74	16.26	3.13	16.74	3.35	17.44	2.92
Cliqueness	19.90	3.00	19.47	4.15	18.87	3.58	19.38	2.60
Satisfaction	19.05	3.77	18.39	3.86	17.79	3.30	18.70	2.53
Disorganisation	15.82	3.96	16.48	4.03	16.01	3.02	16.70	3.30
Competitiveness	21.68	2.54	21.81	2.82	22.01	2.81	21.58	3.00
Innovation	18.59	3.84	17.31	3.60	17.21	3.45	18.12	2.85

Classroom Learning Environment in Four Types of Schools

Table 6.3 presents the perception of the students studying in Aided, Government, Kendriya and Public Schools in respect of sixteen dimensions of learning environment. The perceptions of the students of the above types of schools have been presented with the help of mean and standard deviation values. There are sixteen dimensions of the learning environment which yield information in respect of the conditions and characteristics of the school providing for learning to the students.

The main components regarding which Mean and S.D. values have been obtained are cohesiveness, diversity, formality speed, material-environment, friction, goal-direction, favouritism, difficulty, apathy, democracy, cliqueness, satisfaction, disorganisation, competitiveness and innovation. A careful study of the table suggests the following observations:

(i) Students studying in Kendriya schools shows better inter-personal relationship than students studying in other schools. The mean cohesiveness score ($\bar{x}$ = 20.68) is marginally higher to the mean cohesiveness scores for Aided ($\bar{x}$ = 19.19), Government ($\bar{x}$ = 18.84) and Public schools ($\bar{x}$ = 20.37). However there seems to be no appreciable variations in the cohesiveness aspect of the learning environment of the four types of schools studies by the investigator.

(ii) The four types of schools seem to have similar level of diversity. The mean values for the diversity component in these schools namely, Aided ($\bar{x}$ = 20.05), Government ($\bar{x}$ = 20.00), Kendriya ($\bar{x}$ = 20.73) and Public ($\bar{x}$ = 20.03) are almost alike. This indicates that institutional activities provided for developing and nurturing students' interests are similar. In fact, students' perception of their schools in respect of diversity learning environment component does not show appreciable variations. This is borne out by the fact that the score ranges between 1.89 to 2.56 which is indeed very low in the context of the smallest mean value of 20.00 observed in the case of Government schools.

(iii) Adherence to the formal rules and conventions is a characteristic feature of all the four type of schools namely, Aided ($\bar{x}$ = 20.68), Government ($\bar{x}$ = 21.04), Kendriya ($\bar{x}$ = 18.71) and Public ($\bar{x}$ = 18.44). However, there is a greater emphasis on conformity to rules in Government and Aided schools in comparison to Kendriya and Public schools.

(iv) Teachers of Aided schools have been perceived by their students to complete their courses with greater speed ($\bar{x}$ = 19.43) than teachers teaching in Government schools ($\bar{x}$ = 18.93), Kendriya Vidyalayas ($\bar{x}$ = 17.72) and Public schools

($\bar{x}$ = 17.11). It seems teaching in Public school is at a optimum level of speed than is the case in other schools.

(v) The material environment in the Kendriya Vidyalayas seems to be much more conducive for learning ($\bar{x}$ = 20.21) than the material-environment obtaining in Aided ($\bar{x}$ = 18.79), Government ($\bar{x}$ = 17.44) and Public ($\bar{x}$ = 18.87).

(vi) There is a relatively greater friction as per perception of the students in Kendriya schools ($\bar{x}$ = 19.18) than in Aided ($\bar{x}$ = 18.55), Government ($\bar{x}$ = 19.09) and Public ($\bar{x}$ = 18.08).

(vii) There is no appreciable difference in the goal-direction aspect of learning environment of the four types of schools, namely, Aided ($\bar{x}$ = 20.82), Government ($\bar{x}$ = 20.25), Kendriya ($\bar{x}$ = 20.72) and Public ($\bar{x}$ = 19.02).

(viii) As far as the question of favouritism by teachers is concerned students of all the four types of schools, Aided ($\bar{x}$ = 17.18), Government ($\bar{x}$ = 17.44), Kendriya ($\bar{x}$ = 17.83) and Public ($\bar{x}$ = 17.02) perceive its magnitude almost alike.

(ix) But for students of Public schools who feel their class work to be relatively more difficult ($\bar{x}$ = 18.53), students of Aided ($\bar{x}$ = 17.18), Government ($\bar{x}$ = 17.43) and Kendriya ($\bar{x}$ = 17.35) feel the class work of their schools to be of almost equal difficulty level.

(x) As far as the question of students apathetic attitude towards class activities is concerned, students of Government ($\bar{x}$ = 15.04) and Public schools ($\bar{x}$ = 16.92) show relatively more apathy towards the class activities than the students of Aided ($\bar{x}$ = 14.68) and Kendriya Vidyalayas ($\bar{x}$ = 14.99).

(xi) It seems there is no appreciable difference among four types of schools, Aided ($\bar{x}$ = 16.74), Government ($\bar{x}$ = 16.26), Kendriya ($\bar{x}$ = 16.74) and Public ($\bar{x}$ = 17.44) in respect of the extent to which the students share the decision-making process in the classroom. The extent of democracy operating in these schools is almost equal.

(xii) Cliqueness is a characteristic feature of all the schools observed in this study. Interestingly the magnitude of cliqueness in Aided ($\bar{x}$ = 19.90), Government ($\bar{x}$ = 19.47), Kendriya ($\bar{x}$ = 18.87) and Public ($\bar{x}$ = 19.38) is almost similar. Each school has students who refuse to mix up with other students of their class. They maintain their separate identity and there by also influence the cohesiveness character of the class.

(xiii) Students of Aided schools derive greater satisfaction ($\bar{x}=19.05$) in the class work than students studying in remaining types of schools, namely Government ($\bar{x}=18.39$), Kendriya ($\bar{x}=17.79$) and Public ($\bar{x}=18.70$). The superiority of the Aided schools over the other schools, however, is just marginal.

(xiv) All types of schools without exception show disorganisation which gets manifested in the confusing type of institutional activities and in poor organisation of the institutional programme. On this learning environment component, institutions namely, Aided ($\bar{x}=15.82$), Government ($\bar{x}=16.48$), Kendriya ($\bar{x}=16.01$) and Public ($\bar{x}=16.70$) have not been found to differ significantly.

(xv) All the four types of schools, Aided ($\bar{x}=21.68$), Government ($\bar{x}=21.81$), Kendriya ($\bar{x}=22.01$) and Public ($\bar{x}=21.58$) are undistinguishable in respect of competitiveness component of learning environment.

(xvi) Innovative practices are reported by the students to be marginally greater in operation in Aided ($\bar{x}=18.59$) and Public schools ($\bar{x}=18.12$) than in Government ($\bar{x}=17.31$) and Kendriya schools ($\bar{x}=17.21$).

Table 6.4 reveals overall significant differences on nine of the sixteen components of learning environment, namely, cohesiveness (F=8.348**), formality (F=18.147**), speed (F=20.093**), material environment (F=11.772**), goal-direction (F=6.636**), difficulty (F=6.385**), apathy (F=7.085**), satisfaction (F=2.770*), and innovation. (F=4.473**). The significant F-values as stated above convincingly demonstrate that the Aided, Government, Kendriya and Public schools differ significantly in respect of their learning environment. In fact, it will not be too far from the truth to state that each type of school has a distinctive learning environment.

Having observed the differences in the learning environment of the above types of schools, it seems worthwhile to compare the learning environment of two institutions at a time. The t-values contained in Table 6.4 yield the following facts:

TABLE 6.4: *F* and *t*-values of Students of Four Types of Schools on Learning Environment Dimensions

Classroom Learning Environment Dimensions	*F*-values	*t*-Values Pertaining to Different Dimensions of Learning Environment of Comparison Groups and Significance Level at 5%(*) and 1%(**)					
		A and G	A and K	A and P	G and K	G and P	K and P
1. Cohesiveness	8.35**	0.83	3.49**	2.56**	4.33**	3.34**	0.70
2. Diversity	2.54	0.16	2.17*	0.07	2.38*	0.10	2.41*
3. Formality	18.15**	0.78	4.46**	5.59**	4.94**	5.85**	0.73
4. Speed	20.09**	1.63	5.04**	6.51**	3.90**	5.60**	1.72
5. M. Environment	11.77**	2.76**	2.95**	0.14	6.63**	2.97**	3.02**
6. Friction	2.27	1.16	1.48	1.41	0.19	2.11*	2.42*
7. Goal-direction	6.64**	1.40	0.23	3.94**	1.18	2.85**	3.85**
8. Favouritism	0.74	0.47	1.22	0.29	0.71	0.74	1.47
9. Difficulty	6.38**	0.80	0.53	4.19**	0.25	3.26**	3.46**
10. Apathy	7.08**	0.73	0.62	4.52**	0.08	3.56**	3.58**
11. Democracy	2.40	1.14	0.00	1.58	1.16	2.98**	1.61
12. Cliqueness	1.82	0.98	2.40*	1.39	1.23	0.21	1.19
13. Satisfaction	2.77*	1.42	2.77**	0.84	1.28	0.75	2.25*
14. Disorganisation	1.44	1.35	0.42	1.83	1.05	0.46	1.57
15. Competitiveness	0.48	0.40	0.95	0.27	0.56	0.60	1.06
16. Innovation	4.47**	2.82**	2.93**	1.02	0.24	1.85	2.08*

(i) Aided schools differ from the Government schools on two dimensions of the learning environment scale, namely, material environment (t=2.76**) and innovation (t=2.82**), five dimensions of the same scale namely, cohesiveness (t=3.49**), formality (t=4.46**), speed (t=5.04**), material-environment (t=2.95**) and innovation (t=2.93**) from the Kendriya schools and six dimensions of the learning environment namely, cohesiveness (t=2.56*), formality (t=5.59**) speed (t=6.51**), goal-direction (t=3.94**), difficulty (t=4.19**), and apathy (t=4.52**) from the public schools.

(ii) Government schools are significantly different from Kendriya Vidyalayas on four components of learning environment namely, cohesiveness (t=4.33**), formality (t=4.94**), speed (t=3.90**) and material-environment (t=6.63**) and also from public schools on seven dimensions of the same scale, namely, cohesiveness (t=3.34**), formality (t=5.85**), speed (t=5.60**), material-environment (t=2.97**), goal-direction (t=2.85**), difficulty (t=3.26**) and apathy (t=3.56**).

(iii) Kendriya Vidyalayas have been found to differ significantly from the public schools on five dimensions of learning environment scale, namely, material-environment (t=3.02**), goal-direction (t=3.85**), difficulty (t=3.46**), apathy (t=3.58**), and innovation (t=2.08*).

(iv) Diversity, friction, favouritism, democracy, cliqueness, satisfaction, disorganisation and competitiveness are the dimensions of the learning environment on which no significant difference has been observed between any of the six pairs of schools, i.e. Aided and Government, Aided and Kendriya, Aided and Public, Government and Kendriya, Government and Public and Kendriya and Public.

From a perusal of mean values on the sixteen dimensions of learning environment for Aided, Government, Kendriya and Public schools, the following additional facts emerge:

1. Material-environment in the Aided schools is better than Government, equal to Public and less better to Kendriya Schools.
2. Innovation factor of the environment scale is more developed

in Aided schools than other types of schools.

3. Cohesiveness is much more in Kendriya and Public schools than in Government and Aided institutions.
4. There is less formality in Kendriya and Public schools and more formality in Government schools. Aided schools occupy the middle position in this regard.
5. There is greater quickness or speed in the completion of class work in Aided schools than in Kendriya and Public schools. Class work completion takes place at a similar speed in Aided and Government schools.
6. Goal-direction is much more manifest in Aided schools than in Public schools. But it is much more manifestable in Kendriya Vidyalayas than in Government and other schools.
7. Students of Kendriya Vidyalayas experience more difficulty than students of Aided schools.
8. Students of Aided schools show less apathy than students of Public schools. In fact, students of public schools are not only more apathetic in comparison to students of Aided schools but also to be students of Government and Kendriya Vidyalayas.

Difference between High and Low Creatives of Different Types of Schools and the Total Sample on Learning Environment Dimensions

Having interpreted the data related to the learning environment in terms of the school administration set-up, it will be our effort to interpret data in respect of the perception of the learning environment dimensions by high and low creatives differentiated against the criterion of school type (Table 6.5) and without being differentiated in terms of this criterion (Table 6.6).

Table 6.5 contains mean and standard deviation values of high and low creatives of four types of schools on sixteen dimensions of learning environment and also records t values between the means of the two groups. Table 6.5 yields following observations:

(i) But for one dimension of learning environment namely, material environment where significant differences have been observed (t=2.64*) between High and low creatives of Aided schools, differences on the remaining fifteen learning environment dimensions have been found to be insignificant.

TABLE 6.5: Mean, S.D. and *t*-values for Four Types of Schools Pertaining to Their High and Low Creatives on Learning Environment Dimensions

Dimensions of Learning Environment	Aided			Government			Kendriya			Public		
	Low, N = 19 High, N = 22			Low, N = 20 High, N = 23			Low, N = 17 High, N = 21			Low, N = 19 High, N = 15		
	Mean	S.D.	*t*-values	Mean	S.D.	*t*-values	Mean	S.D.	*t*-values	Mean	S.D.	*t*-values
1	2	3	4	5	6	7	8	9	10	11	12	13
Cohesiveness	L 20.26	4.03	1.47	L 18.05	3.28	0.56	L 20.70	2.68	0.04	L 18.05	2.09	0.63
	H 18.41	4.04		H 18.78	4.96		H 20.67	3.15		H 18.66	3.56	
Diversity	L 20.58	1.95	0.64	L 20.40	3.01	0.18	L 20.76	2.51	0.68	L 20.58	1.54	0.57
	H 20.18	2.01		H 22.56	2.89		H 21.28	2.21		H 20.26	1.66	
Formality	L 20.10	3.16	1.44	L 20.55	4.51	1.70	L 18.82	3.59	0.72	L 19.10	1.82	2.61*
	H 20.45	4.03		H 22.65	3.58		H 18.05	3.07		H 17.53	1.64	
Speed	L 19.68	2.54	0.11	L 19.35	2.92	1.22	L 17.47	2.42	0.54	L 18.16	2.73	1.62
	H 19.59	2.92		H 18.43	1.95		H 17.95	2.99		H 16.80	1.97	
M. Environment	L 20.79	4.06	2.64*	L 16.90	3.46	0.81	L 20.00	2.64	0.42	L 18.68	3.12	1.07
	H 17.00	4.98		H 17.82	3.92		H 20.38	2.92		H 17.46	3.52	
Friction	L 18.42	2.34	0.57	L 21.05	4.02	2.60*	L 20.41	3.20	0.96	L 19.10	2.10	0.73
	H 18.95	3.43		H 17.74	4.27		H 19.43	3.10		H 19.80	3.44	

(*Contd.*)

TABLE 6.5 (*Contd.*)

1	2	3	4	5	6	7	8	9	10	11	12	13
Goal Direction	L 22.05	3.91	1.28	L 20.90	2.78	0.85	L 19.82	2.65	1.60	L 18.26	2.23	0.44
	H 20.50	3.84		H 19.91	4.47		H 21.24	2.75		H 17.80	3.87	
Favouritism	L 17.26	3.74	0.63	L 16.85	3.96	0.56	L 18.23	3.71	0.23	L 19.21	3.32	2.37*
	H 16.45	4.39		H 17.69	5.63		H 17.95	3.80		H 16.40	3.58	
Difficulty	L 17.26	2.72	0.43	L 15.90	2.51	2.88**	L 16.59	2.23	1.62	L 18.95	2.22	0.43
	H 17.59	2.19		H 18.13	2.54		H 17.81	2.38		H 18.60	2.47	
Apathy	L 14.84	4.42	0.34	L 15.30	3.58	0.66	L 15.65	3.96	0.05	L 18.47	3.45	0.83
	H 15.27	3.58		H 14.47	4.41		H 15.57	4.68		H 17.46	3.56	
Democracy	L 17.26	2.55	0.39	L 16.10	2.99	0.45	L 15.94	3.27	0.78	L 17.26	2.92	0.76
	H 16.82	4.40		H 16.56	3.67		H 16.81	3.50		H 16.53	2.58	
Cliqueness	L 20.31	2.86	1.11	L 20.65	2.72	1.29	L 18.12	3.63	1.22	L 19.89	2.05	0.93
	H 19.23	2.35		H 18.91	5.47		H 19.62	3.89		H 20.60	2.35	
Satisfaction	L 19.73	3.66	1.13	L 19.05	3.10	.60	L 18.17	3.57	0.39	L 18.89	1.66	2.96**
	H 18.41	3.83		H 18.35	4.36		H 17.76	3.03		H 16.60	2.82	
Disorganisation	L 14.95	3.52	1.72	L 16.75	3.09	1.47	L 16.53	3.04	0.44	L 17.31	2.38	1.91
	H 16.91	3.75		H 15.09	4.15		H 16.14	2.41		H 19.00	2.75	
Competitiveness	L 21.57	2.41	0.82	L 22.05	2.60	0.85	L 21.82	3.28	1.18	L 21.16	3.32	0.79
	H 22.23	2.61		H 21.26	3.36		H 22.86	2.10		H 21.93	2.05	
Innovation	L 19.31	3.84	0.43	L 19.10	2.82	2.73*	L 18.17	3.35	0.62	L 17.47	2.79	0.09
	H 18.73	4.78		H 16.30	3.74		H 17.52	3.12		H 17.40	1.88	

(ii) The insignificance of difference between high and low creatives of Aided schools implies that high and low creatives of Aided schools perceive their learning environment alike. This is understandable in the context of the fact that each institution has a distinctive type of learning environment and it being same, therefore, it will be perceived as such by all the students whether they are most or least creative. Moreover, perception is a mental function governed by intelligence. There is no perfect relationship between creativity and intelligence. As such a least creative may be highly intelligent and a highly creative may be least intelligent. The similarity of the perception of the learning environment by both these groups needs to be understood in the context of this theoretical position.

(iii) Significant differences have been observed between high and low creatives on three dimensions; friction ($t=2.60$*), difficulty ($t=2.88$**) and innovation (2.73*). On the remaining dimensions differences between these two groups have not found to be significant. This implies that on a considerable majority of dimensions of learning environment, the perception of the high and low creatives of the Government schools is similar. This observation lands strong support to the earlier observation made in the preceding paragraph. As far as the question of the difference between high and low creatives on friction and innovation dimensions of environment is concerned, the low creatives find greater tension and quarrelling among students of their class (L, $\bar{x}=21.05$ and H, $\bar{x}=17.14$) than the high creatives. In this context, two facts need to be noted. The first being that both the groups experience tension in the class. The difference between them is only in the magnitude of tension.

The low creatives feel more tension, because they are not able to find outlet for expression of their potentials. Highly creatives on the other hand feel less tension because of their divergent thinking are able to find more outlets than the low creatives. The perception of greater amount of innovation by low creatives ($\bar{x}=19.10$) than by high creatives ($\bar{x}=16.30$) is possibly because the former group perceive any new activity in the school or classroom as innovative. The latter group, however, does not find any newness in these activities because these are just one form of the same category of activities. The high creatives are able to make such perception because of their divergent thinking. Finally the low creatives find less difficulty ($\bar{x}$=15.90) than the high creatives ($\bar{x}$=18.13). The experience of the difficulty is a function of interest and involvement in the learning task. The high creatives feel classroom activities to be stereo-typed and therefore do not feel interested. Owing to less interest in the learning task given in the classroom, they do not cope with the learning task. Hence they begin to experience more difficulty.

(iv) High and low creatives of Kendriya Vidyalayas have been found to perceive similarly all the dimensions of learning environment. The similarity of their perception need to be understood in the context of explanation already given.

(v) High and low creatives of Public schools have been found to differ significantly on three dimensions of learning environment, namely, formality (t=2.61*), favouritism (t=2.37*) and satisfaction (t=2.96**). On the remaining thirteen dimensions of learning environment, they have not been found to differ significantly.

The low creatives have been found to perceive more formality ($\bar{x}$=19.10) than the high creatives ($\bar{x}$=17.53). Similarly the former creative group finds their teachers to show more favour of some students than to other students of the class ($\bar{x}$=19.21) in comparison to the perception of the high creatives ($\bar{x}$=16.40) regarding such behaviour of the teachers. In fact, the low creatives derive greater satisfaction in their classroom work ($\bar{x}$=18.89) than the high creatives ($\bar{x}$=16.60) in this regard. Teaching in classroom in Public schools follows a specific routine and methodology. There are little variations in the teaching treatments and therefore the highly creatives find little in the class to enthuse and motivate them. As such teaching-learning process for them is a boring job and therefore, they do not derive as much satisfaction as their counterpart do.

Table 6.6 contains Mean and S.D. values of high and low creatives of total sample on sixteen dimensions of learning environment and also records t-values between the means of the two groups.

(i) The observations drawn in Table 6.5 find ample vindication from the data contained in Table 6.6. t-values have been found to be significant only on two dimensions of learning environment scale, speed (t=2.37*) and difficulty (t=2.78**). On the remaining fourteen dimensions of the scale, no significant difference has been observed betwen the high and low creatives of the total sample selected for the purposes of this study. The low creatives according to the mean data find their class work to be covered quickly ($\bar{x}$=18.84) in comparison to the high creatives of the total sample ($\bar{x}$=17.83). The difference in the perception of these two groups on the speed of completion of their class work needs to be looked in their learning goals. Since the low creatives maintain their speed of learning commensurate with the speed of their teaching, therefore they maintain the required pace of classroom work. The high creatives on the other hand owing to their feeling of boredom in class teaching begin to experience gaps in their learnings. The learning gaps retard the speed of their class work.

TABLE 6.6: Mean, S.D. and t-Values Pertaining to High and Low Creatives of Total sample on Learning Environment Dimensions

Learning Environment Dimensions	Low Creatives N = 73		High Creatives N = 80		t-Values
	Mean	S.D.	Mean	S.D.	
Cohesiveness	18.92	3.26	19.79	4.09	1.44
Diversity	20.34	2.56	20.79	2.22	1.14
Formality	20.47	3.78	19.94	3.65	0.87
Speed	18.84	2.68	17.83	2.55	2.37*
M. Environment	19.14	3.86	18.94	3.76	0.32
Friction	19.33	3.44	18.50	3.86	1.39
Goal Direction	20.64	3.26	20.29	3.90	0.61
Favouritism	17.42	3.65	17.22	4.44	0.30
Difficulty	16.86	2.54	17.98	2.37	2.78**
Apathy	15.51	3.81	15.26	4.14	0.38
Democracy	16.74	3.03	17.04	3.54	0.55
Cliqueness	20.00	2.82	19.26	4.10	1.28
Satisfaction	19.19	3.17	18.15	3.44	1.93
Disorganisation	16.21	3.08	16.22	3.37	0.04
Competitiveness	21.64	2.79	22.21	2.48	1.33
Innovation	18.63	3.46	17.84	3.43	1.41

(ii) The above observation find further support from the significance of difference observed between the low and high creatives on difficulty dimension. The high creatives experience more difficulty in the learning task ($\bar{x}=17.98$) than the low creatives ($\bar{x}=17.98$) than the low creatives ($\bar{x}=16.86$). This behaviour on the part of the former group occurs because of its less involvement in the teaching-learning task. A divergent thinker finds challenge only in nonconventional teaching learning activities. The routine academic schedule hardly motivates him. Motivation is a basic condition for learning. In its absence many gaps in learning takes place which ultimately give rise to the feeling of difficulty.

Relationship of Verbal Creativity (A and B), Non-verbal Creativity and Total Creativity with Learning Environment Dimensions in Different Types of Schools and in Total Sample

After comparing the high and low creatives perception of the various dimensions of learning environment, data indicative of the relationship between verbal creativity (A) (Table 6.7), and B (Table 6.8), non-verbal creativity (Table 6.9) and total creativity (Table 6.10) on the one hand and classroom learning environment dimensions on the other has been ascertained through correlation obtained as in school types and in total sample (Table 6.11). *r* values will be interpreted table-wise.

Verbal Creativity A and Learning Environment in School Types

Table 6.7 yields the following observations:

(i) Relationship between verbal creativity (A) and learning environment dimensions is rather low.
(ii) The relationship between verbal creativity (A) and most of the learning environment dimensions is of a negative type.
(iii) There is no dimension which may be designated as significantly related with verbal creativity (A) in more than one type of institution. The significance of the correlates differ from school to school.

TABLE 6.7: *r*-Values between Learning Environment Dimensions and Verbal Creativity-A in Four types of Schools

Learning Environment Dimensions	*r*-Values obtained from sample belonging to Types of Schools			
	Aided	Government	Kendriya	Public
1. Cohesiveness	−.117	.082	.061	.319**
2. Diversity	−.054	−.085	.116	.003
3. Formality	−.129	.081	−.105	−.071
4. Speed	−.011	−.146	.031	−.169
5. M. Environment	−.219**	.052	.002	.012
6. Friction	−.021	−.208**	−.006	−.235*
7. Goal-direction	−.046	−.088	.099	.219*
8. Favouritism	−.119	.030	−.007	−.224*
9. Difficulty	−.002	.193	.148	.178
10. Apathy	−.044	−.011	−.055	−.059
11. Democracy	.003	.045	.037	.017
12. Cliqueness	−.115	−.079	.127	−.125
13. Satisfaction	−.053	−.060	−.074	−.083
14. Disorganisation	.078	−.029	.010	−.097
15. Competitiveness	.103	−.033	.207*	.316**
16. Innovation	−.010	−.215**	.015	−.039

(iv) Verbal creativity bears a low negative relationship with material environment dimension in Aided schools (r=−.219**), with friction (r=-.208**) and innovation (r=-.215**) in Government schools and positive low relationship with competitiveness (r=.207*) in Kendriya schools and negative relationship with friction (r=-.235*) and favouritism (r=-.224*) and positive relationship with cohesiveness (r=.319**), goal-direction (r=.219*) and with competitiveness (r=.316**) in Public schools.

(v) The more is the verbal creativity (A), the lesser is the material environment conducive to learning, the greater is the feeling of friction, innovation and favouritism.

(vi) The more is the verbal creativity (A), the greater is the cohesiveness, goal-direction and competitiveness in the schools.

Verbal creativity — A is a composite of fluency, flexibility and originality components. All these components have much common variances and therefore bear close relationship. A person who shows fluent, flexible and original behaviour will very likely be less satisfied with the type of material-environment of the school, conditions conducive to innovation, experience greater friction, will feel more strongly the effects of teacher favouritism, will perceive greater goal-direction and will feel happier in a competitive situation demanding the use of his total mental abilities for meeting the challenges adequately.

Verbal Creativity B and Learning Environment in School Types

Verbal creativity (B) is a composite of five components. These are fluency, flexibility, originality, elaboration verbal and originality verbal. The correlational values obtained between this variable and learning environment dimensions in all the four types of schools are presented in Table 6.8 and have been found to bear the same characteristic features which has been described and interpreted in the preceding table. It is proposed to avoid repetition of the earlier observations and to concentrate on new observations.

Results, as contained in Table 6.8, yield following observations:

(i) Difficulty dimension is the only dimension which has been found to have relationship with verbal creativity (B) in Government schools. Correlation between these two variables has been found to be rather low (*r*=.197*), although positive. It implies that those who have a highly developed verbal ability perceive greater difficulty with the work of their class than those who has developed less verbal creativity (B). This needs to be examined in the context of the earlier explanation based on the psychology of motivation of divergent thinkers.

(ii) Cliqueness is another dimension which did not bear relationship with verbal creativity (A) but bears it with verbal creativity (B) (*r*=.180*). The relationship between these variables has been observed in Kendriya Vidyalayas alone. The correlation suggests that the divergent thinkers or those who have high verbal creativity (B) tend not to mix-up with other students of their class.

TABLE 6.8: *r*-values between Learning Environment Dimensions and Verbal Creativity-B in Four Types of Schools

Dimensions of Learning Environment	*r*-Values and Their Significance Level Types of Schools			
	Aided	Government	Kendriya	Public
1. Cohesiveness	−.109	.058	.005	.242*
2. Diversity	−.011	−.032	.158	.065
3. Formality	−.140	.150	−.071	−.032
4. Speed	−.001	−.101	.073	−.131
5. M. Environment	−.210**	.030	.010	.010
6. Friction	.058	−.264**	−.009	−.114
7. Goal-direction	−.105	−.063	.136	.102
8. Favouritism	−.094	.056	.040	−.169
9. Difficulty	.029	.197*	.151	.063
10. Apathy	.042	−.038	−.037	−.064
11. Democracy	−.038	.045	.071	.017
12. Cliqueness	−.114	−.141	.180*	−.072
13. Satisfaction	−.069	−.058	−.011	−.170
14. Disorganisation	.138	−.087	.004	.009
15. Competitiveness	.068	−.056	.245**	.227*
16. Innovation	−.030	−.268**	.035	−.024

Non-Verbal Creativity and Learning Environment in School Types

Non verbal creativity is a composite of elaboration non-verbal and originality non-verbal. School typewise correlational values obtained between non-verbal creativity and learning environment dimensions are reported in Table 6.9 and present the following factual situation:

(i) By and large non-verbal creativity bears a negative relationship with the learning dimensions.
(ii) The magnitude of their relationship is rather low.
(iii) There are very few dimensions of learning environment with which non-verbal creativity holds significant relationship.
(iv) The nature of correlation and the type of significant correlates differ from school to school.
(v) In Aided schools non-verbal creativity holds negative but low correlation with material environment (r=-.257**) and low positive relationship with difficulty (r=.183*) and disorganisation (r=.186*).
(vi) The more developed is the non-verbal creativity, the lesser conducive is the material environment, the more intense is the

feeling of difficulty and greater is the perception of disorganisation in the aided school.

(vii) Friction is the only learning environment component which has been found to bear a negative low relationship (r=-.219**) with non-verbal creativity and that too in only one school, namely Government.

(viii) In Kendriya Vidyalayas the observation is that non-verbal creativity does not bear significant relationship with many of the sixteen dimensions of learning environment.

(ix) In Public schools four dimensions of learning environment, formality, goal-direction, satisfaction and disorganisation have been found to be related to non-verbal creativity. Three of these four components bear low negative relationship with non-verbal creativity and one bears a positive relationship. The negatively related components are formality (r=-.258**), goal-direction (r=-.209*) and satisfaction (-.207*). Disorganisation bears a positive relationship with non-verbal creativity (r=.279**).

TABLE 6.9: *r*-Values between Learning Environment Dimensions and Non-verbal Creativity in Four Types of Schools

Dimensions of Learning Environment	*r* Values and Their Significance Level Types of Schools			
	Aided	Government	Kendriya	Public
1. Cohesiveness	–.122	.024	.081	–.089
2. Diversity	–.003	.038	.041	.172
3. Formality	–.096	.139	–.058	–.258**
4. Speed	–.016	–.056	–.011	–.094
5. Material Environment	–.257**	.022	.014	–.140
6. Friction	.110	–.219**	–.051	.089
7. Goal-direction	–.121	.108	–.035	–.209*
8. Favouritism	.006	.006	.014	–.094
9. Difficulty	.183*	.016	.107	–.184
10. Apathy	.036	–.158	.022	–.061
11. Democracy	–.026	.078	–.005	–.178
12. Cliqueness	–.071	–.101	–.037	.062
13. Satisfaction	–.099	.064	–.019	–.207*
14. Disorganisation	.186*	–.136	.009	.279**
15. Competitiveness	.020	–.001	.045	–.125
16. Innovation	–.044	–.035	–.126	–.022

Total Creativity and Learning Environment in School Types

Total creativity, it is needless to say, is a composite of such components as fluency, flexibility, originality, elaboration verbal, originality verbal, elaboration non-verbal and originality non-verbal. The correlational values contained in Table 6.10 indicate the following inferences:

(i) Like the correlation between verbal creativity (A and B), non-verbal creativity and classroom learning environment dimensions, the correlation between total creativity and learning environment dimensions is also low and generally negative.

(ii) In Aided schools creativity bears a negative low relationship with material environment (r=-.246**) and positive low relationship with disorganisation (r=.167*).

(iii) In Government schools creativity has been found to be negatively correlated with friction (r=-.283**) and innovation (r=-.227**) and positive relationship with formality (r=.166*) and difficulty (r=.165*).

(iv) In Kendriya Vidyalayas only one learning environment dimension; competitiveness has been found to be positively related with total creativity (r=.197*) of the students.

(v) In Public schools satisfaction is the only learning environment component which has been found to be significantly related with total creativity (r=-.209*). However the relationship between these variables is negative.

(vi) With differences in school, the learning environment dimensions holding significant relationship with creativity also differ. This implies that school administrative set-up is a significant factor which influences the relationship between learning environment and creativity.

Creativity and Learning Environment in Total Sample

After placing the factual position of the relationship between creativity and its three types; verbal creativity (A), verbal creativity (B) and non-verbal creativity on the one hand and learning environment dimensions on the other in school types, it is proposed to examine and interpret the correlational values that have been obtained by correlating the same sets of the variables but on the total sample of the students belonging to all the four types of schools. Table 6.11 contains the correlational values obtained after correlating the sets of variables already mentioned. A careful glance of the correlation values leads to the following findings:

(i) Creativity as well as its components bear low relationship with a considerably large number of learning environment dimensions.

(ii) The trend pertaining to the magnitude of relationship between the creativity components and learning environment components converge either towards insignificance or towards a low relationship.

(iii) Verbal creativity (A and B) are related in a large number of cases with the same learning environment components, namely, friction (VCA*r*=-.106*, VCB*r*=-.094*), difficulty (VCA*r*=.115** and VCB*r*=.127**), competitiveness (VCA*r*=.138** and VCB*r*=.112*) and innovation (VCA*r*=-.088* and VCB*r*=-.106*).

TABLE 6.10: *r*-Values between Learning Environment Dimensions and Total Creativity in Four Types of Schools

Dimensions of Learning Environment	*r*-Values and their Significance Level TYPES OF SCHOOLS			
	Aided	Government	Kendriya	Public
1. Cohesiveness	−.124	.054	.036	.156
2. Diversity	−.009	−.013	.132	.114
3. Formality	−.140	.166*	−.075	−.121
4. Speed	−.006	−.099	.049	−.137
5. M. Environment	−.246**	.031	.013	−.043
6. Friction	.080	−.283**	−.027	−.056
7. Goal-direction	−.121	−.017	−.085	.003
8. Favouritism	−.073	.047	.035	−.167
9. Difficulty	.080	.165*	.153	−.019
10. Apathy	.045	−.081	−.018	−.073
11. Democracy	−.038	.061	.049	−.053
12. Cliqueness	−.112	−.146	.116	−.033
13. Satisfaction	−.086	−.027	−.016	−.209*
14. Disorganisation	.167*	−.114	.006	.110
15. Competitiveness	.060	−.045	.197*	.131
16. Innovation	−.037	−.227**	−.025	−.027

TABLE 6.11: *r*-Values between Learning Environment Dimensions on the One Hand and Verbal Creativity A, Verbal Creativity B, Non-verbal Creativity and Total Creativity of the Total Sample on the Other

Dimensions of Learning Environment	*r*-Values and their Significance Level			
	Verbal Creativity (A)	Verbal Creativity (B)	Non-verbal Creativity	Total Creativity
1. Cohesiveness	.079	.071	.044	.070
2. Diversity	−.003	.047	.074	.063
3. Formality	−.046	−.044	−.117**	−.076
4. Speed	−.076	−.088*	−.132**	−.114*
5. M. Environment	−.035	−.026	−.028	−.030
6. Friction	−.106*	−.094*	−.040	−.086
7. Goal-direction	.038	−.007	−.079	−.034
8. Favouritism	−.057	−.023	−.006	−.020
9. Difficulty	.115**	.127**	.061	.120**
10. Apathy	−.049	−.008	−.005	−.008
11. Democracy	.018	.026	−.001	.020
12. Cliqueness	−.057	−.062	−.069	−.072
13. Satisfaction	−.079	−.086	−.065	−.089*
14. Disorganisation	−.006	.018	.069	.039
15. Competitiveness	.138**	.112*	−.009	.083
16. Innovation	−.088*	−.106*	−.071	−.107*

(iv) Verbal creativity (B) in addition to holding significant relationship with the aforesaid learning environment dimensions, holds significant relationship with speed (*r*=-.088*).

(v) Non-verbal creativity is significantly related to formality (*r*=-.117**) and speed (*r*=-.132**) only.

(vi) Total creativity is also related to speed (*r*=-.114*), difficulty (*r*=.120**), satisfaction (*r*=-.089*) and innovation (*r*=-.107*). Speed, difficulty, satisfaction and innovation are those characteristics of the learning environment which either facilitate or retard the growth of creativity. Growth of creativity requires an environment which does not encourage the teachers or the students to complete their teaching and learning assignments quickly. The more a teacher or student resorts to the speed of completion of the course, the more is the possibility of the implementation of a convergent type of teaching. The latter type of teaching leaves little scope for divergent thinking and therefore puts a premium on the growth of creativity.

Similarly if the teacher presents the learning task of a difficulty level commensurate to the pupils intellectual level, they will be able to think as many solutions to the problems as come to their mind and such a situation needless to say will encourage the development of creativity.

Satisfaction from class work influences creativity but negatively. The reason being that the growth of creativity requires some amount of dissatisfaction against the conditions obtaining in the school environment. When there is a dissatisfaction against the routine type of student responses and teacher's teaching situations, the learner feels motivated to go beyond the data presented by the teacher and think new solutions to a problem, develop new hypotheses, establish new equations and derive further problems from the original ones. The net result of these behaviours and environmental condition is that creativity develops.

Finally, innovation is also a condition which influences the development of creativity.

Prediction Effectiveness of Learning Environment Dimensions in respect of— (a) Verbal A (b) Verbal B (c) Non-Verbal and (d) Total Creativity, in Different Types of Schools and for the Total Sample

In the present study the influence of the learning environment dimensions on creativity and its components has been sought to be studied through several statistical procedures, as for example, central tendencies, dispersion, analysis of variance, test of significance and correlation. Determination of regression co-efficients is the other statistical method through which the influence of learning environment dimensions on creativity has been examined. In fact regression is the only statistical method which can help in predicting the occurrence of a particular behaviour cognitive, psychomotor or affective. Creativity is a cognitive ability which is influenced by learning environment. This observation gets support not only from earlier research but also from the *F*, *t* and *r*-values obtained in this study.

The investigator with a view to ascertain the role of environment in creativity development sought to find out regression co-efficients for each of the sixteen dimensions of learning environment and in reference to their value in predicting verbal (A and B), non-verbal and total creativity. To examine the predictability of the learning environment dimensions independent of the influence of school administration type, the regression co-efficients were determined separately for each school. Besides this exercise, regression co-efficients were also calculated on the basis of total sample of the study. It is proposed to interpret the regression co-efficients of a particular learning environment dimension creativity component wise. This proposition will enable us to compare regression co-efficients of several schools at one time. The interpretation will be made under the following heads:

A. Learning environment dimensions and verbal creativity (A) in school types and in total sample.
B. Learning environment dimensions and verbal creativity (B) in school types and in total sample.
C. Learning environment dimensions and non-verbal creativity in school types and in total sample.
D. Learning environment dimensions and total creativity in school types and in total sample.

A. *Learning Environment Dimensions and Verbal Creativity (A) in School Types and in Total Sample*

Tables 6.12 to 6.16 yield the following information:

(i) Most of the learning environment dimensions do not have the ability to predict the verbal creativity (A). This observation holds true for all types of schools as well as for the total sample,
(ii) The above observation implies that although learning environment influences creativity, it cannot be used as a valid predictor of creativity. In fact, the influence on creativity is exerted by the total environment which contains dynamic forces acting, reacting and interacting. The interplay of these forces gives the environment a unique entity which as a whole influences the growth of creativity. When environment is

segmented and differentiated into specific components its gestalt pattern gets lost, and

(iii) For each one of the sixteen learning environment dimensions differ from school to school. The learning environment dimensions which have been found to have significant regression co-efficients in one school have not been found to have the same in other schools. As for example material-environment, cliqueness and favouritism have been found to have significant regression co-efficients in Aided schools. But in Government schools such learning environment components have been found to have significant regression co-efficients as innovation, friction, speed, difficulty and cohesiveness.

TABLE 6.12: Stepwise Multiple Regression Analysis of Classroom Learning Environment Dimensions and Significant Predictors of Verbal Creativity (A) in Aided Schools N = 130

Classroom Climate Dimensions	Regression Coefficient	S.E. of Reg. Coefficient	Multiple R	R^2	Increment in R^2	F-Ratio
Material Environment	−2.2487	0.8139	0.2186	0.0478	0.0478	7.633**
Cliqueness	−2.4276	1.1634	0.3356	0.1126	0.0648	4.354**
Favouritism	−1.4279	0.6567	0.3821	0.1460	0.0333	4.728**
Competitiveness	1.1911	1.0082	0.3991	0.1593	0.0133	1.396
Satisfaction	−0.5778	1.0163	0.4091	0.1673	0.0080	0.323
Apathy	−1.2173	0.9195	0.4189	0.1755	0.0082	1.752
Disorganisation	0.8331	0.8564	0.4269	0.1822	0.0067	0.946
Cohesiveness	−0.7240	0.9460	0.4308	0.1856	0.0033	0.586
Formality	−0.6431	0.9562	0.4342	0.1885	0.0029	0.452
Friction	−0.4996	0.8793	0.4362	0.1903	0.0018	0.323
Innovation	0.3470	0.8727	0.4377	0.1916	0.0012	0.158
Goal Direction	0.3682	0.9110	0.4389	0.1926	0.0010	0.163
Democracy	−0.2342	0.8043	0.4396	0.1932	0.0006	0.085
Diversity	0.1088	0.9980	0.4396	0.1933	0.0001	0.012
Speed	−0.1007	0.9244	0.4397	0.1934	0.0001	0.012

Intercept = 278.409

TABLE 6.13: Stepwise Multiple Regression Analysis of Classroom Learning Environment Variables and Significant Predictors of Verbal Creativity (A) in Government Schools N = 140

Classroom Climate Variables	Regression Coefficient	S.E. of Reg. Coefficient	Multiple R	R^2	Increment in R^2	F-Ratio
Innovation	−1.3902	0.7246	.2155	.0464	.0464	3.681**
Friction	−2.1928	0.8310	.3035	.0921	.0457	6.693**
Speed	−3.2101	1.0125	.3717	.1381	.0460	10.052**
Difficulty	1.6842	0.9441	.4176	.1744	.0363	3.182**
Formality	0.9887	0.7390	.4288	.1839	.0094	1.790*
Favouritism	0.3273	0.6204	.4358	.1899	.0060	0.278
Cohesiveness	1.1911	0.8344	.4445	.1975	.0076	2.038*
Cliqueness	0.7818	0.9066	.4513	.2037	.0062	0.744
Goal Direction	−0.6323	0.9652	.4549	.2070	.0033	0.429
M. Environment	0.7218	0.8112	.4584	.2101	.0031	0.792
Satisfaction	−0.6738	0.8765	.4625	.2139	.0038	0.591
Disorganisation	0.4891	0.8769	.4652	.2164	.0025	0.311
Apathy	−0.3198	0.7434	.4666	.2177	.0013	0.185
Diversity	−0.5010	0.9800	.4679	.2189	.0012	0.261
Competitiveness	0.3045	0.8359	.4688	.2197	.0008	0.133

Intercept = 196.275

TABLE 6.14: Stepwise Multiple Regression Analysis of Classroom Learning Environment Dimensions and Significant Predictors of Verbal Creativity (A) in Kendriya Vidyalayas N = 112

Classroom Climate Variables	Regression Coefficient	S.E. of Reg. Coefficient	Multiple R	R^2	Increment in R^2	F-Ratio
Competitiveness	2.0882	0.9172	0.2108	0.0444	0.0444	5.183**
Difficulty	1.9474	1.0299	0.2764	0.0764	0.0320	3.576**
Formality	−1.0519	0.9229	0.2917	0.0851	0.0087	1.299
Apathy	−0.4438	0.8407	0.3182	0.1012	0.0161	0.279
Cliqueness	2.0543	0.9234	0.3401	0.1156	0.0144	4.949**
Friction	−1.4202	1.0917	0.3682	0.1356	0.0200	1.692
Cohesiveness	1.4119	1.0013	0.3861	0.1491	0.0135	1.988*
Diversity	1.1269	1.1629	0.3953	0.1563	0.0072	0.939
Democracy	0.7290	1.0026	0.4013	0.1611	0.0048	0.529
Satisfaction	−0.5902	1.0437	0.4040	0.1632	0.0021	0.320
Speed	−0.4741	1.0378	0.4068	0.1655	0.0023	0.209
Innovation	−0.1940	0.8752	0.4074	0.1660	0.0005	0.049
Favouritism	−0.1328	0.7651	0.4077	0.1663	0.0003	0.030
Disorganisation	−0.1469	1.0340	0.4080	0.1664	0.0001	0.020

Intercept = 52.713

TABLE 6.15: Stepwise Multiple Regression Analysis of Classroom Learning Environment Variables and Significant Predictors of Verbal Creativity (A) in Public Schools N = 98

Classroom Climate Variables	Regression Coefficient	S.E. of Reg. Coefficient	Multiple R	R^2	Increment in R^2	F-Ratio
Cohesiveness	0.8033	1.1374	0.3194	0.1020	0.1020	0.499
Competitiveness	2.6898	1.0861	0.3950	0.1560	0.0540	6.134**
Formality	−1.0611	1.6850	0.4394	0.1930	0.0370	0.397
Favouritism	−1.9095	0.8492	0.4716	0.2224	0.0294	5.056**
Satisfaction	−2.1784	1.2429	0.4995	0.2495	0.0271	3.072**
Friction	−1.8953	1.2348	0.5122	0.2624	0.0129	2.356**
Democracy	−1.2690	1.1886	0.5257	0.2764	0.0140	1.140
Innovation	−0.6223	1.0586	0.5372	0.2885	0.0121	0.346
Disorganisation	1.2778	1.3100	0.5424	0.2942	0.0057	0.951
Goal Direction	0.7566	1.3270	0.5472	0.2995	0.0053	0.325
Cliqueness	−0.7001	1.2604	0.5497	0.3022	0.0027	0.308
M. Environment	−0.3948	0.9157	0.5517	0.3044	0.0022	0.186
Difficulty	0.7219	1.4260	0.5529	0.3057	0.0013	0.256
Speed	−0.6297	1.3674	0.5545	0.3074	0.0017	0.212
Diversity	−0.4270	1.5280	0.5550	0.3080	0.0006	0.078
Apathy	−0.1388	0.9302	0.5552	0.3082	0.0002	0.022

Intercept = 226.094

TABLE 6.16: Stepwise Multiple Regression Analysis of Classroom Learning Environment Dimensions and Significant Predictors of Verbal Creativity (A) in Total sample N = 480

Classroom Climate Variables	Regression Coefficient	S.E. of Reg. Coefficient	Multiple R	R^2	Increment in R^2	F-Ratio
Competitiveness	1.5576	0.4538	0.1384	0.0191	0.0191	11.778**
Friction	−1.0839	0.4475	0.1823	0.0332	0.0141	5.866**
Satisfaction	−1.1697	0.4762	0.2416	0.0584	0.0252	6.034**
Speed	−1.0661	0.4682	0.2574	0.0662	0.0078	5.184**
Difficulty	1.1073	0.4975	0.2743	0.0753	0.0091	4.953**
Apathy	−0.6322	0.4016	0.2846	0.0810	0.0057	2.478**
Innovation	−0.7133	0.3934	0.2969	0.0881	0.0071	3.287**
Favouritism	−0.5537	0.3362	0.3062	0.0938	0.0057	2.712**
Cohesiveness	0.4113	0.4515	0.3085	0.0952	0.0014	0.830
M. Environment	−0.4105	0.3895	0.3123	0.0975	0.0023	1.111
Diversity	0.1712	0.5248	0.3126	0.0977	0.0002	0.106
Formality	−0.1154	0.4325	0.3129	0.0979	0.0002	0.071
Goal Direction	0.1869	0.4978	0.3132	0.0981	0.0002	0.141
Cliqueness	−0.1226	0.4896	0.3134	0.0982	0.0001	0.063
Disorganisation	0.1090	0.4736	0.3136	0.0983	0.0001	0.053

Intercept = 185.441

Competitiveness, difficulty, cliqueness and cohesiveness are the learning environment dimensions found to have significant regression co-efficients in Kendriya schools. In Public schools three learning environment dimensions, namely, favouritism, satisfaction and friction have emerged as significant predictors of verbal creativity (A). However, in the total sample competitiveness, friction, satisfaction, speed, difficulty, apathy, innovation and favouritism have been found to have significant regression co-efficients.

(iv) Tables 6.12 to 6.16 reveal a steady and systematic increase in the value of correlation with systematic addition of new learning environment dimensions as independent variables and verbal creativity (A) as dependent variable.

(v) In Aided schools consequent to the increment of influence of sixteen learning environment components 19.34 per cent of its common variance with verbal creativity (A) can be explained. This is indeed a low percentage keeping in view the fact that influence of sixteen independent variables has been accounted for. In fact out of 19.34 per cent total variance explained by the total number of learning environment variables, the major contribution (14.59%) to it is made by three factors, namely, material-environment (4.78%), cliqueness (6.48%), favouritism (3.33%). The individual contribution of each one of these three factors to total variance is indeed rather small. But there is no doubt that each one of them has some predictive effectiveness; although it may be rather low.

(vi) In Government schools sixteen learning environment dimensions explain 21.97 per cent total variance. To this explained variance a contribution of 18.20 per cent variance is made by five factors, namely, innovation (4.64%), friction (4.57%), speed (4.60%), difficulty (3.63%) and cohesiveness (0.76%).

(vii) In Kendriya schools a total of 16.64 per cent of the variance is explained by sixteen variables of learning environment. Out of 16.64 per cent explained variance, a contribution of 10.43 per cent is made to it by four factors, namely competitiveness (4.44%), difficulty (3.20%), cliqueness (1.44%) and cohesiveness (1.35%).

(viii) An examination of the Table 6.15 reveals that a total of 30.82 per cent of the variance is explained by all the variables of learning environment in public schools. Four factors, namely competitiveness, favouritism, satisfaction and friction which have significant *F*-values explain 5.40 per cent, 2.94 per cent, 2.71 per cent and 1.29 per cent variance respectively.

(ix) In total sample a total of 9.83 per cent of the variance is explained by the sixteen variables of learning environment. The factors which have significant F-values are competitiveness, friction, satisfaction, speed, difficulty, apathy, innovation and favouritism.

B. *Learning Environment Dimensions and Verbal Creativity (B) in School Types and in Total Sample*

Tables 6.17 to 6.21 yield the following information:

(i) Tables 6.17 to 6.21 summarise results of step-wise regression analysis with verbal creativity (B) as the criterion variable and learning environment component scores as the predictor variables. The tables give Regression co-efficients, Multiple R, R^2, increment in R^2, percentage of variance explained and corresponding F-values.

(ii) Most of the learning environment dimensions do not have the ability to predict the verbal creativity (B). This observation holds true for all types of schools as well as for the total sample.

(iii) An examination of Table 6.17 reveals that out of sixteen components of learning environment, three factors namely, material environment, cliqueness and favouritism turn out to be significant predictors of verbal creativity (B) in Aided schools explaining the percentage variance to the tune of 4.42, 6.20 and 2.30 respectively. The sixteen components of learning environment put together explain only 17.07 per cent of variance leaving a large part of variance unexplained.

(iv) It can be seen in Table 6.18 that in Government schools 26.62 per cent variance is explained by sixteen components of learning environment put together of which a major part (25.36%) is contributed by six factors, namely, friction (6.95%), innovation (7.18%), speed (3.40%), formality (3.41%), favouritism (2.46%) and difficulty (1.96%). The individual contribution of each one of these six factors to total variance is indeed rather small. But there is no doubt that each one of them has some predictive value, although it may be rather low.

TABLE 6.17: Stepwise Multiple Regression Analysis of Classroom Learning Environment Dimensions and Significant Predictors of Verbal Creativity (B) in Aided Schools N = 130

Classroom Climate Dimensions	Regression Coefficient	S.E. of Reg. Coefficient	Multiple R	R^2	Increment in R^2	F-Ratio
M. Environment	–2.4542	1.0711	0.2102	0.0442	0.0442	5.250**
Cliqueness	–4.1449	1.5309	0.3258	0.1062	0.0620	7.330**
Favouritism	–1.5411	0.8642	0.3595	0.1292	0.0230	3.180**
Disorganisation	1.3726	1.1270	0.3872	0.1499	0.0207	1.483
Competitiveness	1.6657	1.3267	0.4023	0.1618	0.0119	1.576
Democracy	–0.6738	1.0584	0.4067	0.1654	0.0035	0.405
Satisfaction	–0.4544	1.3374	0.4084	0.1668	0.0014	0.115
Innovation	0.4857	1.1484	0.4100	0.1681	0.0013	0.179
Formality	–0.5064	1.2583	0.4109	0.1689	0.0008	0.162
Speed	0.3864	1.2164	0.4117	0.1695	0.0006	0.101
Friction	0.2337	1.1571	0.4123	0.1700	0.0005	0.041
Diversity	0.2582	1.3134	0.4127	0.1703	0.0003	0.039
Cohesiveness	–0.1972	1.2448	0.4129	0.1705	0.0002	0.025
Apathy	–0.1763	1.2101	0.4130	0.1706	0.0001	0.021
Goal Direction	–0.1230	1.1988	0.4131	0.1707	0.0001	0.011

Intercept = 350.837

TABLE 6.18: Stepwise Multiple Regression Analysis of Classroom Learning Environment Dimension and Significant Predictors of Verbal Creativity (B) in Government Schools N = 140

Classroom Climate Variables	Regression Coefficient	S.E. of Reg. Coefficient	Multiple R	R^2	Increment in R^2	F-Ratio
Friction	–3.5603	1.1454	0.2637	0.0695	0.0695	9.661**
Innovation	–2.3052	0.9988	0.3758	0.1413	0.0718	5.326**
Speed	–4.1588	1.3956	0.4187	0.1753	0.0340	8.880**
Formality	2.1057	1.0186	0.4576	0.2094	0.0341	4.274**
Favouritism	1.2480	0.8551	0.4837	0.2340	0.0246	2.130*
Difficulty	1.8784	1.3014	0.5036	0.2536	0.0196	2.083*
Satisfaction	–1.1795	1.2082	0.5089	0.2590	0.0054	0.953
Apathy	–0.5020	1.0247	0.5166	0.2617	0.0027	0.240
Cohesiveness	0.5154	1.1501	0.5131	0.2632	0.0015	0.201
Diversity	0.7293	1.3508	0.5145	0.2648	0.0016	0.292
M. Environment	0.3240	1.1181	0.5150	0.2652	0.0004	0.084
Goal Direction	–0.3014	1.3304	0.5154	0.2656	0.0004	0.051
Disorganisation	0.3253	1.2087	0.5157	0.2659	0.0003	0.072
Cliqueness	–0.2167	1.2496	0.5159	0.2661	0.0002	0.030
Competitiveness	–0.1439	1.1522	0.5160	0.2662	0.0001	0.016

Intercept = 344.217

TABLE 6.19: Stepwise Multiple Regression Analysis of Classroom Learning Environment Dimenions and Significant Predictors of Verbal Creativity (B) in Kendriya Vidyalayas N = 112

Classroom Climate Variables	Regression Coefficient	S.E. of Reg. Coefficient	Multiple R	R^2	Increment in R^2	F-Ratio
Competitiveness	3.4280	1.4358	0.2480	0.0615	0.0615	5.700**
Difficulty	3.7397	1.5618	0.3095	0.0958	0.0343	5.733**
Cliqueness	3.9429	1.3521	0.3335	0.1112	0.0154	8.504**
Friction	−3.5462	1.5638	0.4156	0.1728	0.0616	5.142**
Diversity	2.1020	1.6317	0.4306	0.1854	0.0126	1.660
Cohesiveness	1.5192	1.4305	0.4437	0.1969	0.0115	1.128
Democracy	1.8002	1.4194	0.4503	0.2027	0.0058	1.609
Formality	−1.3954	1.3262	0.4618	0.2133	0.0106	1.107
Favouritism	0.9494	1.1045	0.4656	0.2168	0.0035	0.739
Innovation	−0.7216	1.2558	0.4676	0.2187	0.0019	0.330
Satisfaction	0.7735	1.5291	0.4704	0.2213	0.0026	0.256
M. Environment	−0.2362	1.4036	0.4705	0.2214	0.0001	0.028
Goal Direction	0.2662	1.6223	0.4707	0.2216	0.0002	0.027
Speed	−0.1930	1.4816	0.4709	0.2217	0.0001	0.017

Intercept = 16.580

TABLE 6.20: Stepwise Multiple Regression Analysis of Classroom Learning Environment Dimensions and Significant Predictors of Verbal Creativity (B) in Public Schools N = 98

Classroom Climate Variables	Regression Coefficient	S.E. of Reg. Coefficient	Multiple R	R^2	Increment in R^2	F-Ratio
Cohesiveness	2.4949	1.7962	0.2416	0.0584	0.0584	1.929*
Satisfaction	−4.5920	1.9629	0.3278	0.1074	0.0490	5.473**
Favouritism	−2.8040	1.3411	0.3752	0.1408	0.0334	4.371**
Competitive notes	3.6556	1.7152	0.4193	0.1758	0.0350	4.543**
Disorganisation	2.9468	2.0688	0.4513	0.2037	0.0279	2.029*
Difficulty	−1.3850	2.2521	0.4598	0.2114	0.0077	0.378
Cliqueness	−0.8774	1.9905	0.4646	0.2158	0.0044	0.194
Diversity	0.7629	2.4131	0.4688	0.2198	0.0040	0.100
Friction	−1.1453	1.9501	0.4725	0.2233	0.0035	0.345
Innovation	−1.1563	1.6718	0.4754	0.2260	0.0027	0.478
Speed	−1.2348	2.1594	0.4769	0.2274	0.0014	0.327
Formality	1.2847	2.6610	0.4786	0.2291	0.0017	0.233
Democracy	−0.4722	1.8772	0.4793	0.2298	0.0007	0.063
M. Environment	0.3165	1.4461	0.4801	0.2304	0.0006	0.048
Goal Direction	−0.6905	2.0957	0.4807	0.2310	0.0006	0.109
Apathy	−0.3776	1.4690	0.4813	0.2317	0.0007	0.066

Intercept = 296.521

TABLE 6.21: Stepwise Multiple Regression Analysis of Classroom Learning Environment Dimensions and Significant Predictors of Verbal Creativity (B) in Total Sample. N = 480.

Classroom Climate Variables	Regression Coefficient	S.E. of Reg. Coefficient	Multiple R	R^2	Increment in R^2	F-Ratio
Difficulty	1.5589	0.7142	0.1257	0.0158	0.0158	4.764**
Competitiveness	1.9400	0.6517	0.1653	0.0273	0.0115	8.860**
Friction	−1.5920	0.6473	0.2008	0.0403	0.0130	6.049**
Satisfaction	−1.4443	0.6884	0.2400	0.0576	0.0173	4.402**
Speed	−1.6856	0.6730	0.2649	0.0702	0.0126	6.272**
Innovation	−1.2826	0.5730	0.2766	0.0765	0.0063	5.011**
Diversity	1.2507	0.7534	0.2857	0.0816	0.0051	2.756**
Cliqueness	−0.6669	0.7072	0.2957	0.0874	0.0058	0.889
Democracy	0.4886	0.6684	0.2987	0.0892	0.0018	0.534
Cohesiveness	0.6238	0.6504	0.3007	0.0904	0.0012	0.920
Favouritism	−0.3490	0.4900	0.3018	0.0911	0.0007	0.507
M. Environment	−0.2836	0.5602	0.3029	0.0917	0.0006	0.256
Apathy	−0.3198	0.5790	0.3036	0.0922	0.0005	0.305
Disorganisation	0.3792	0.6798	0.3045	0.0927	0.0005	0.311
Formality	0.2261	0.6209	0.3048	0.0929	0.0002	0.133
Goal Direction	−0.2174	0.7145	0.3051	0.0931	0.0002	0.093

Intercept = 267.775

(v) An examination of Table 6.19 reveals that in Kendriya schools 22.17 per cent variance is explained by sixteen components of learning environment. A major contribution (17.28%) to the above variance is made by four factors, namely, competitiveness (6.15%), difficulty (3.43%), cliqueness (1.54%) and friction (6.16%). Although the individual contribution of each one of these four factors to total variance is small but there is no doubt about their predictive effectiveness.

(vi) Table 6.20 presents results in respect of variance (23.17%) explained by all learning environment components in Public schools. A major contribution (20.37%) to the above variance is made by four factors, namely, cohesiveness (5.84%), satisfaction (4.90%), favouritism (3.34%), and competitiveness (3.50%). The individual contribution of each one of these four factors is indeed rather small. But there is no doubt that each one of them has some predictive effectiveness, although it may be rather low.

(vii) Table 6.21 reveals that seven factors, namely, difficulty, competitiveness, friction, satisfaction, speed, innovation and diversity, out of sixteen components of learning environment turn out to be significant predictors of verbal creativity (B) in total sample, explaining 1.58 per cent, 1.15 per cent, 1.30 per cent, 1.73 per cent, 1.26 per cent, 0.63 per cent and 0.51 per cent variance respectively. The variance (9.31%) explained by all the sixteen dimensions put together is small leaving a large part of variance unexplained.

C. *Learning Environment Dimensions and Non-verbal Creativity in School Types and in Total Sample*

Tables 6.22 to 6.26 yield the following information:

(i) Tables 6.22 to 6.26 give Regression co-efficients, multiple R, R^2, increment in R^2, variance explained and *F*-values emerging from the stepwise regression analysis for the prediction of non-verbal creativity of students of four types of schools, namely, Aided, Government, Kendriya and Public and the total sample.

TABLE 6.22: Stepwise Multiple Regression Analysis of Classroom Learning Environment Dimensions and Significant Predictors of Non-Verbal Creativity in Aided Schools. N = 130.

Classroom Climate Dimensions	Regression Coefficient	S.E. of Reg. Coefficient	Multiple R	R^2	Increment in R^2	F-Ratio
Material Environment	−1.1086	0.4001	0.2571	0.0661	0.0661	7.678**
Cliqueness	−1.3321	0.5896	0.3422	0.1171	0.0510	5.105**
Disorganisation	0.6808	0.4466	0.3778	0.1427	0.0256	2.324*
Difficulty	0.8166	0.6047	0.3855	0.1486	0.0058	1.824
Favouritism	−0.5156	0.3563	0.3998	0.1598	0.0112	2.094*
Apathy	−0.3116	0.4767	0.4063	0.1651	0.0052	0.427
Speed	−0.2376	0.4808	0.4102	0.1682	0.0031	0.244
Formality	0.2344	0.4968	0.4127	0.1703	0.0021	0.223
Satisfaction	−0.2789	0.5128	0.4148	0.1720	0.0017	0.296
Competitiveness	0.1759	0.5193	0.4164	0.1734	0.0013	0.115
Friction	0.1529	0.4479	0.4177	0.1745	0.0011	0.117
Innovation	0.1136	0.4419	0.4185	0.1752	0.0006	0.066
Diversity	0.0718	0.5122	0.4187	0.1753	0.0001	0.020
Goal Direction	0.0601	0.4659	0.4188	0.1754	0.0001	0.017

Intercept = 124.558

TABLE 6.23: Stepwise Multiple Regression Analysis of Classroom Learning Environment Dimensions and Significant Predictors of Non-Verbal Creativity in Government Schools N = 140

Classroom Climate Variables	Regression Coefficient	S.E. of Reg. Coefficient	Multiple R	R^2	Increment in R^2	F-Ratio
Friction	−1.2361	0.4944	0.2188	0.0479	0.0479	6.252**
Diversity	0.6613	0.5805	0.2563	0.0658	0.0178	1.298
Speed	−1.1875	0.5982	0.2914	0.0849	0.0192	3.941**
Favouritism	0.5881	0.3729	0.3075	0.0946	0.0096	2.487**
Formality	0.3544	0.4371	0.3306	0.1093	0.0147	0.657
Apathy	−0.5632	0.4561	0.3394	0.1152	0.0059	1.525
M. Environment	−0.4926	0.4832	0.3523	0.1241	0.0089	1.039
Cohesiveness	−0.4961	0.5001	0.3593	0.1291	0.0049	0.984
Goal-Direction	0.7661	0.5772	0.3706	0.1374	0.0082	1.762*
Competitiveness	−0.2869	0.4956	0.3749	0.1405	0.0031	0.335
Difficulty	0.3545	0.5629	0.3787	0.1434	0.0029	0.396
Innovation	−0.2095	0.4291	0.3807	0.1449	0.0015	0.238
Disorganisation	−0.2208	0.5252	0.3815	0.1456	0.0007	0.177
Cliqueness	0.2096	0.5461	0.3826	0.1464	0.0008	0.147
Democracy	0.1896	0.6113	0.3835	0.1470	0.0006	0.096
Satisfaction	−0.668	0.5186	0.3836	0.1472	0.0002	0.017

Intercept = 123.345

TABLE 6.24: Stepwise Multiple Regression Analysis of Classroom Learning Environment Variables and Significant Predictors of Non-Verbal Creativity in Kendriya Vidyalayas. N = 112.

Classroom Climate Variables	Regression Coefficient	S.E. of Reg. Coefficient	Multiple R	R^2	Increment in R^2	F Ratio
Innovation	−1.5919	0.7533	0.1258	0.0158	0.0158	4.465**
Cohesiveness	1.3984	0.8762	0.1807	0.0326	0.0168	2.547**
Diversity	1.2823	1.0143	0.2178	0.0474	0.0148	1.598
Difficulty	1.5462	0.9380	0.2370	0.0562	0.0087	2.717**
M. Environment	0.6768	0.8506	0.2488	0.0619	0.0057	0.633
Apathy	0.6160	0.7595	0.2609	0.0680	0.0061	0.658
Friction	−1.1556	0.9456	0.2754	0.0758	0.0078	1.494
Competitiveness	1.0976	0.8646	0.2914	0.0849	0.0091	1.612
Goal Direction	−0.8590	1.0027	0.2982	0.0889	0.0040	0.734
Satisfaction	0.6413	0.9285	0.3059	0.0935	0.0046	0.477
Favouritism	0.5021	0.6607	0.3121	0.0974	0.0039	0.577
Democracy	0.4038	0.8695	0.3162	0.1000	0.0026	0.216
Cliqueness	0.1743	0.8156	0.3169	0.1004	0.0004	0.046
Speed	−0.1890	0.8969	0.3175	0.1008	0.0004	0.044
Disorganisation	−0.1165	0.8962	0.3178	0.1010	0.0002	0.017
Formality	0.0857	0.8041	0.3180	0.1011	0.0001	0.011

Intercept = 17.196

TABLE 6.25: Stepwise Multiple Regression Analysis of Classroom Learning Environment Variables and Significant Predictors of Non-Verbal Creativity in Public Schools. N = 98.

Classroom Climate Variables	Regression Coefficient	S.E. of Reg. Coefficient	Multiple R	R^2	Increment in R^2	F-Ratio
Disorganisation	1.4620	0.8813	0.2794	0.0781	0.0781	2.752**
Favouritism	−1.7757	0.5986	0.3743	0.1001	0.0620	8.799**
Apathy	−1.3143	0.6465	0.4089	0.1672	0.0271	4.132**
Goal Direction	−1.7970	0.9198	0.4698	0.2207	0.0535	3.817**
Democracy	−1.1685	0.8371	0.4914	0.2414	0.0207	1.948*
Friction	−0.6966	0.8696	0.5020	0.2520	0.0106	0.642
Satisfaction	−1.2108	0.8754	0.5150	0.2652	0.0132	1.913
Difficulty	−1.1813	0.9688	0.5242	0.2748	0.0096	1.487
Diversity	1.0991	1.0786	0.5305	0.2815	0.0067	1.038
Cohesiveness	0.4737	0.8073	0.5350	0.2862	0.0047	0.344
Competitiveness	0.4646	0.7574	0.5379	0.2894	0.0032	0.376
Formality	−0.7071	1.1673	0.5405	0.2921	0.0027	0.367
Speed	0.1863	0.9517	0.5408	0.2924	0.0003	0.038
Cliqueness	0.1071	0.8832	0.5409	0.2926	0.0002	0.015

Intercept = 211.187

TABLE 6.26: Stepwise Multiple Regression Analysis of Classroom Learning Environment Dimensions and Significant Predictors of Non-Verbal Creativity in Total Sample N = 480

Classroom Climate Variables	Regression Coefficient	S.E. of Reg. Coefficient	Multiple R	R^2	Increment in R^2	F-Ratio
Speed	−0.8685	0.3173	0.1316	0.0173	0.0173	7.494**
Formality	−0.3025	0.2930	0.1552	0.0241	0.0068	1.066
Cliqueness	−0.5543	0.3318	0.1876	0.0352	0.0111	2.792**
Diversity	0.7966	0.3556	0.2138	0.0457	0.0105	5.018**
Difficulty	0.3794	0.3371	0.2271	0.0516	0.0059	1.267
Innovation	−0.3265	0.2666	0.2358	0.0556	0.0040	1.501
Apathy	−0.3708	0.2721	0.2406	0.0579	0.0023	1.857*
Goal Direction	−0.4414	0.3373	0.2468	0.0609	0.0030	1.713
Cohesiveness	0.3034	0.3059	0.2510	0.0630	0.0021	0.983
Disorganisation	0.3547	0.3209	0.2548	0.0649	0.0019	1.222
Friction	−0.3449	0.3032	0.2595	0.0673	0.0024	1.294
Satisfaction	−0.1677	0.3226	0.2605	0.0678	0.0005	0.270
Competitiveness	0.1509	0.3075	0.2614	0.0683	0.0005	0.241
Favouritism	−0.0612	0.2278	0.2616	0.0684	0.0001	0.072
M. Environment	−0.0505	0.2639	0.2618	0.0685	0.0001	0.037

Intercept = 126.977

(ii) Most of the learning environment dimensions do not have the ability to predict the non-verbal creativity. This observation holds true for all types of schools as well as for the total sample.

(iii) For each one of the sixteen learning environment dimensions differ from school to school. The learning environment dimensions which have been found to have significant regression co-efficients in one school have not been found to have the same in other schools. As for example material-environment, cliqueness and disorganisation have been found to have significant regression co-efficients in Aided schools. But in Government schools such learning environment components have been found to have significant regression co-efficients as friction, speed and favouritism. Innovation, cohesiveness and difficulty are the learning environment dimensions found to have significant regression co-efficients in Kendriya schools. In Public schools five learning environment dimensions, namely, disorganisation, favouritism, apathy, goal-direction and democracy have emerged as significant predictors of non-verbal creativity. However, in the total sample speed, cliqueness, diversity and apathy have been found to have significant regression co-efficients.

(iv) Consequent to the increment of influence of sixteen learning environment components 17.54 per cent of its common variance with non-verbal creativity in Aided schools, 14.72 per cent in Govt. Schools, 10.11 per cent in Kendriya schools, 29.26 per cent in Public schools and 6.85 per cent in total sample can be explained. This is indeed a low percentage keeping in view the fact that influence of sixteen independent variables has been accounted for. In fact out of 17.54 per cent total variance explained by the total number of learning environment variables in Aided schools, the major contribution (14.27%) to it is made by three factors, namely material-environment (6.61%), cliqueness (5.10%) and disorganisation (2.56%).

In Government schools, out of 14.72 per cent total variance explained by the sixteen learning environment variables, the major part (7.67%) to it is contributed by three factors, namely, friction

(4.79%), speed (1.92%) and favouritism (0.96%).

In Kendriya schools, out of 10.11 per cent variance explained by the sixteen variables of learning environment, 4.13 per cent of it is contributed by three factors, namely, innovation (1.58%), cohesiveness (1.68%) and difficulty (0.87%).

In Public schools out of 29.26 per cent total variance explained by the total number of learning environment variables, the major contribution (24.14%) to it is made by five factors, namely, disorganisation (7.81%), favouritism (6.20%), apathy (2.71%), goal-direction (5.35%) and democracy (2.07%).

In total sample, a very small variance 6.85 per cent is explained by sixteen dimensions of learning environment of which 4.12 per cent is contributed by four factors, namely, speed (1.73%), cliqueness (1.11%), diversity (1.05%) and apathy (0.23%).

The Individual Contribution of each one of these factors to total variance is indeed rather small. But there is no doubt that each one of them has some predictive value, although it may be rather low.

(D) *Learning Environment Dimensions and Total Creativity in School Types and in Total Sample*

Tables 6.27 to 6.31 yield the following information:

(i) Tables 6.27 to 6.31 give Regression co-efficients, multiple R, R^2, increment in R^2, Percentage variance explained and *F*-values emerging from the step-wise regression analysis for the prediction of total creativity of students of four types of schools and total sample.

(ii) Most of the learning environment dimensions do not have the ability to predict the total creativity. This observation holds true for all types of schools as well as for the total sample.

(iii) In Aided schools consequent to the increment of influence of sixteen learning environment components 19.72 per cent of its common variance with total creativity can be explained. This is indeed a low percentage. Out of 19.72 per cent variance explained by the total number of learning environment variables, the major contribution (17.82%) to it is made by four factors, namely, material-environment (6.05%), cliqueness (7.12%), disorganisation (2.55%), favouritism (2.10%).

TABLE 6.27: Stepwise Multiple Regression Analysis of Classroom Learning Environment Dimensions as Significant Predictors of Total Creativity in Aided Schools N = 130

Classroom Climate Variables	Regression Co-efficient	S.E. of Reg. Co-efficient	Multiple R	R^2	Increment in R^2	F-Ratio
Material Environment	−3.5963	1.3312	0.2459	0.0605	0.0605	7.298**
Cliqueness	−5.4887	1.9074	0.3629	0.1317	0.0712	8.280**
Disorganisation	2.0748	1.4206	0.3965	0.1572	0.0255	2.133*
Favouritism	−2.0369	1.1528	0.4222	0.1782	0.0210	3.122**
Competitiveness	1.8199	1.5811	0.4354	0.1895	0.0113	1.325
Democracy	−0.6640	1.3211	0.4375	0.1914	0.0018	0.253
Innovation	0.6010	1.4329	0.4329	0.1930	0.0016	0.176
Satisfaction	−0.7459	1.6622	0.4412	0.1946	0.0016	0.201
Difficulty	0.7151	1.9186	0.4420	0.1954	0.0008	0.139
Friction	0.3878	1.4411	0.4428	0.1960	0.0006	0.072
Apathy	−0.4548	1.5282	0.4434	0.1966	0.0006	0.089
Diversity	0.3321	1.6272	0.4437	0.1969	0.0003	0.042
Formality	−0.2637	1.5768	0.4439	0.1970	0.0001	0.028
Cohesiveness	−0.1689	1.5332	0.4440	0.1971	0.0001	0.012
Speed	0.1560	1.5382	0.4441	0.1972	0.0001	0.010

Intercept = 475.125.

TABLE 6.28: Stepwise Multiple Regression Analysis of Classroom Learning Environment Dimensions as Significant Predictors of Total Creativity in Government Schools N = 140

Classroom Climate Variables	Regression Co-efficient	S.E. of Reg. Co-efficient	Multiple R	R^2	Increment in R^2	F-Ratio
Friction	−4.7736	1.2669	0.2827	0.0799	0.0799	14.197**
Innovation	−2.5199	1.2280	0.3655	0.1336	0.0537	4.211**
Speed	−5.3426	1.7180	0.4119	0.1697	0.0361	9.670**
Formality	2.4195	1.1119	0.4520	0.2043	0.0346	4.735**
Favouritism	1.8524	1.0317	0.4830	0.2333	0.0290	3.224**
Difficulty	2.2408	1.5837	0.4963	0.2463	0.0130	2.002*
Diversity	1.3905	1.6546	0.5022	0.2522	0.0059	0.706
Apathy	−1.0612	1.2925	0.5059	0.2559	0.0037	0.674
Satisfaction	−1.2564	1.4705	0.5103	0.2605	0.0046	0.730
Competitiveness	−0.4181	1.4088	0.5108	0.2609	0.0004	0.088
Goal Direction	0.4656	1.6004	0.5112	0.2613	0.0004	0.085
Democracy	0.2133	1.6686	0.5113	0.2614	0.0001	0.016
Material Environment	−0.1746	1.3718	0.5114	0.2615	0.0001	0.016

Intercept = 469.082.

TABLE 6.29: Stepwise Multiple Regression Analysis of Classroom Learning Environment Dimensions as Significant Predictors of Total Creativity in Kendriya Schools N = 112

Classroom Climate Variables	Regression Co-efficient	S.E. of Reg. Co-efficient	Multiple R	R^2	Increment in R^2	F-Ratio
Competitiveness	4.5189	2.0570	0.1988	0.0395	0.0395	4.826**
Difficulty	5.3001	2.2338	0.2684	0.0720	0.0325	5.630**
Friction	–4.7279	2.2303	0.2947	0.0869	0.0149	4.494**
Cliqueness	4.1102	1.9402	0.3485	0.1214	0.0345	4.488**
Diversity	3.3871	2.3832	0.3625	0.1314	0.0100	2.020*
Cohesiveness	2.9417	2.0862	0.3778	0.1427	0.0113	1.988*
Innovation	–2.3083	1.7860	0.3921	0.1537	0.0110	1.670
Democracy	2.2372	2.0417	0.3984	0.1587	0.0050	1.201
Formality	–1.2853	1.8968	0.4050	0.1640	0.0053	0.459
Favouritism	1.4490	1.5703	0.4112	0.1691	0.0051	0.851
Satisfaction	1.4413	2.1738	0.4153	0.1725	0.0034	0.440
Apathy	0.6843	1.7977	0.4176	0.1744	0.0019	0.145
Material Environment	0.4659	2.0093	0.4181	0.1748	0.0004	0.054
Goal Direction	–0.5707	2.3862	0.4187	0.1753	0.0005	0.057
Speed	–0.3706	2.1347	0.4190	0.1756	0.0003	0.030

Intercept = 28.164.

TABLE 6.30: Stepwise Multiple Regression Analysis of Classroom Learning Environment Dimensions as Significant Predictors of Total Creativity in Public Schools N = 98

Classroom Climate Variables	Regression Co-efficient	S.E. of Reg. Co-efficient	Multiple R	R^2	Increment in R^2	F-Ratio
Satisfaction	–5.7996	2.4821	0.2092	0.0438	0.0438	5.459**
Favouritism	–4.5852	1.6959	0.3291	0.1083	0.0645	7.310**
Competitiveness	4.1330	2.1689	0.3646	0.1329	0.0246	3.631**
Disorganisation	4.3836	2.6161	0.4052	0.1642	0.0313	2.808**
Cohesiveness	2.9714	2.2713	0.4458	0.1987	0.0345	1.711
Apathy	–1.6977	1.8576	0.4646	0.2158	0.0171	0.835
Difficulty	–2.5926	2.8478	0.4737	0.2243	0.0085	0.829
Democracy	–1.6373	2.3737	0.4799	0.2303	0.0060	0.476
Friction	–1.8521	2.4660	0.4868	0.2370	0.0067	0.564
Goal Direction	–2.5052	2.6500	0.4919	0.2420	0.0050	0.894
Diversity	1.8510	3.0514	0.4963	0.2463	0.0043	0.368
Innovation	–1.2060	2.1141	0.4992	0.2492	0.0029	0.325
Speed	–1.0542	2.7306	0.5002	0.2502	0.0010	0.149
Cliqueness	–0.7568	2.5171	0.5009	0.2509	0.0007	0.090
Formality	0.5950	3.3649	0.5012	0.2512	0.0003	0.031
Material Environment	0.2871	1.8286	0.5014	0.2514	0.0002	0.025

Intercept = 510.074.

TABLE 6.31: Stepwise Multiple Regression Analysis of Classroom Learning Environment Dimensions as Significant Predictors of Total Creativity in Total Sample N = 480

Classroom Climate Variables	Regression Co-efficient	S.E. of Reg. Co-efficient	Multiple R	R^2	Increment in R^2	F-Ratio
Difficulty	1.9287	0.9215	0.1176	0.0138	0.0138	4.380**
Speed	−2.5749	0.8458	0.1750	0.0306	0.0168	9.268**
Friction	−1.9456	0.8353	0.2060	0.0424	0.0118	5.425**
Satisfaction	−1.6254	0.8821	0.2328	0.0542	0.0118	3.395**
Competitiveness	2.0913	0.8460	0.2568	0.0659	0.0117	6.110**
Diversity	2.0437	0.9773	0.2696	0.0727	0.0068	4.373**
Innovation	−1.6159	0.7403	0.2835	0.0803	0.0076	4.765**
Cliqueness	−1.2218	0.9180	0.2987	0.0892	0.0089	1.772*
Cohesiveness	0.9365	0.8386	0.3014	0.0908	0.0016	1.247
Disorganisation	0.7587	0.8426	0.3043	0.0926	0.0018	0.811
Apathy	−0.6802	0.7435	0.3060	0.0936	0.0010	0.837
Goal Direction	−0.6711	0.9186	0.3075	0.0946	0.0010	0.534
Favouritism	−0.4110	0.6360	0.3093	0.0956	0.0010	0.418
Democracy	0.4861	0.8675	0.3101	0.0962	0.0006	0.314
M. Environment	−0.3369	0.7266	0.3108	0.0966	0.0004	0.215

Intercept = 394.007.

(iv) In Government schools, out of 26.15 per cent total variance explained by the sixteen learning environment variables, the major contribution (24.63%) to it is made by six factors, namely, friction (7.99%), innovation (5.37%), speed (3.61%), formality (3.46%), favouritism (2.90%), and difficulty (1.30%).

(v) In Kendriya schools, out of 17.56 per cent total variance explained by the total number of learning environment variables, a major part (14.27%) of it is contributed by six factors, namely, competitiveness (3.95%), difficulty (3.25%), friction (1.49%), cliqueness (3.45%), diversity (1.00%) and cohesiveness (1.13%).

(vi) Table 6.30 reveals that the sixteen variables are able to explain 25.14 per cent of the variance in total creativity in Public schools. Four variables, namely, satisfaction (4.38%), favouritism (6.45%), competitiveness (2.46%) and disorganisation (3.13%) contribute a major part (16.42%) to the above total variance (25.14%) explained.

(vii) In total sample, the Table 6.31 reveals that only 9.66 per cent of the variance is explained by sixteen components of learning environment, leaving a major variance unexplained. The predictors which have significant *F*-values are difficulty, speed, friction, satisfaction, competitiveness, diversity, innovation and cliqueness.

The individual contribution of each one of these factors to total variance is indeed rather small. But there is no doubt that each one of them has some predictive effectiveness, although it may be rather low.

A comparative study of the variances of the tables of total sample and those observed in the four types of schools, brings tolight the significant differences in the size of explained variances between the two. The explained variances in respect of the total dimensions of learning environment hardly exceeds 10 per cent in total sample. Whereas the variance size in different schools ranges between 17 per cent to 31 per cent. This makes an interesting study. One possible reason for the low size of variance in the total sample is the regression effect phenomenon. The second possible reason emanates from the fact that schools have different classroom learning environment. When individual reactions to the learning environment of the class are lumped together, then the group or class or school effect naturally gives way. However, notwithstanding the relative low proportion of total variance, the number of factors having significant regression co-efficient is greater in the total sample than in individual school.

SECTION C

Teachers' Perception of an Ideal Pupil and Creativity

One of the most powerful ways in which a culture encourages or discourages creative behaviour is the way by which teachers and parents encourage or discourage, reward or punish certain personality characteristics as they develop in children or the behaviours which manifest those characteristics. 'It has been pointed out that what parents, teachers and society encourage and discourage seems to be more important than heritability' (Dehlevi and Torrance, 1979). It has been recognised that teachers play an important role in encouraging or discouraging creative potential of the children.

Since teacher attitudes and values seem to be of considerable significance in the emergence and development of creative thinking, it would be fruitful to study the qualities that teachers of four types of schools, namely, Aided, Government, Kendriya and Public — like to encourage and conversely condemn and discourage in their children. If we could determine what characteristics teachers encourage and discourage, we would be able to understand and predict creative achievements more accurately. Such information would provide useful clues for helping individuals to achieve their potential and for helping teachers to facilitate creative growth among children. Therefore, the present section is concerned with answering the following questions:

1. What do teachers of four types of schools believe are the most desirable and least desirable traits of an ideal child?
2. Do teachers of Aided, Government, Kendriya and Public schools differ in their perceptions?
3. How do the perceptions of these four types of schools compare with those of the "Creativity experts"?

Perception of Teachers of Aided, Government, Kendriya and Public Schools

Tables 6.32 to 6.35 yield the following information in respect of teachers' perceptions about ideal pupils in four types of schools, namely, Aided, Government, Kendriya and Public.

(i) A study of the ten most valued traits by teachers of Aided, Government, Kendriya and Public schools points to one significant finding, that there are nine common characteristics which appear in four types of schools (Table 6.32). The teachers of these schools have given a high place to characteristics such as doing work on time, courteous, remembering well, industrious, considerate of others, altruistic, healthy, obedient, curious, energetic, vigorous, sincere and self-confident.

(ii) There is also considerable agreement between the kinds of behaviours, the teachers of four types of schools believe should be discouraged. There are almost nine common characteristics which appear in four types of schools namely, Aided, Government, Kendriya and Public, and there is not much difference in the ranks assigned to the ten least valued traits by the teachers of the above schools (Table 6.33). The teachers of these schools want to discourage such characteristics as negativistic, fault-finding, spirited in disagreement, disturbing, timid and bashful, guessing and critical of others.

(iii) The results in Table 6.34 indicate the rank order coefficients of correlation between the perceptions of the teachers of four types of schools on ten most valued traits of an ideal pupil. The correlations came out to be .76 between teachers of Aided and Government schools, .84 between Aided and Kendriya, .80 between Aided and Public, .77 between Government and Kendriya, .86 between Government and Public, .84 between Kendriya and Public schools which are quite high and significant. This indicates that there is a great deal of agreement between the perception of teachers from four types of schools on the qualities of an ideal child which they like most and want to see and develop in their pupils.

(iv) Table 6.35 presents the rank order correlation coefficients between the perception of the teachers from four types of schools on ten least valued traits of an ideal child, the correlations being .90 between Aided and Government school teachers, .87 between Aided and Kendriya school teachers, .87 between Aided and Public school teachers, .93 between Government and Kendriya school teachers, .90 between Government and Public school teachers and .94 between Kendriya and Public school teachers, which are quite high and significant. The analysis of results indicates that there is quite close agreement between the perception of teachers from the above categories of schools on the characteristics of an ideal pupil which they like and value least, and do not want to see and develop in their students.

Table 6.36 presents the correlations between teachers' perceptions of an ideal pupil in four types of schools and ratings of experts on creative personality.

Relationship between Teachers' Perception and Creativity Experts' Nomination

The results in Table 6.36 indicate that the teachers of four types of schools namely, Aided, Government, Kendriya and Public and

TABLE 6.32: The Most Valued Traits of the Ideal Pupil as Perceived by the Teachers of Four Types of Schools

Ranks	Aided	Government	Kendriya	Public
1.	Curious, Searching	Courteous, Polite	Doing work on time	Courteous, Polite
2.	Courteous, Polite	Healthy	Courteous, Polite	Healthy
3.	Healthy	Remembering well	Curious, Searching	Curious, Searching; Independent in thinking
4.	Doing work on time	Curious, Searching	Healthy	Doing work on time
5.	Industrious, busy	Doing work on time, Obedient	Remembering well	Altruistic, Remembering well
6.	Remembering well	Industrious, busy	Altruistic	Self-Confident
7.	Considerate of others, Desirous of excelling	Self-Confident	Affectionate, Considerate of others	Industrious, Busy
8.	Altruistic, Independent in judgement	Altruistic	Industrious, busy	Independent in judgement
9.	Self-Confident	Independent in Judgement, Physically strong	Independent in judgement; Self-Confident	Affectionate, Considerate of others
10.	Energetic, Vigorous; Obedient	Energetic, Vigorous, Neat and Orderly	Energetic, Vigorous; Sincere	Energetic, Vigorous; Sincere

TABLE 6.33: The Least Valued Traits of the Ideal Pupil as Perceived by the Teachers of the Four Types of Schools — Aided, Government, Kendriya and Public

Ranks	Aided	Government	Kendriya	Public
1.	Fearful, apprehensive	Fearful, apprehensive	Fearful, apprehensive	Fearful, apprehensive
2.	Stubborn	Stubborn, Disturbing procedures and organisation of the group	Stubborn, Disturbing procedures and organisation of the group	Stubborn
3.	Disturbing procedures and organisation of the group	Talkative	Timid, shy and bashful	Critical of others; fault finding
4.	Talkative	Timid, shy and bashful	Critical of others; Fault finding	Disturbing procedures and organisation of the group; Talkative
5.	Timid, shy and bashful	Negativistic	Talkative	Timid, shy and bashful
6.	Fault-finding	Fault-finding	Negativistic	Negativistic
7.	Negativistic	Spirited in disagreement	Haughty	Haughty
8.	Liking to work alone	Domineering	Liking to work alone	Domineering
9.	Spirited in disagreement	Guessing; Liking to work alone	Guessing	Liking to work alone
10.	Domineering	Emotionally sensitive	Emotionally sensitive	Guessing

TABLE 6.34: *r*-Values between Most Valued Traits of the Ideal Pupils as Perceived by the Teachers of Four Types of Schools

Types of Schools	Aided	Government	Kendriya	Public
Aided	—	.76	.84	.80
Government	—	—	.77	.86
Kendriya	—	—	—	.84
Public	—	—	—	—

TABLE 6.35: *r*-Values between Least Valued Traits of the Ideal Pupils as Perceived by the Teachers of Four Types of Schools

Types of Schools	Aided	Government	Kendriya	Public
Aided	—	.90	.87	.87
Government	—	—	.93	.90
Kendriya	—	—	—	.94
Public	—	—	—	—

TABLE 6.36: Correlation between the Rankings of Teachers' Perceptions of Four Types of Schools and Experts on Creative Personality

Types of Schools	*r* Values between Teachers' perception and Experts on Creative Personality
Aided	.04
Government	.03
Kendriya	.09
Public	.07

experts on creative personality view the ideal child in quite different ways. There are only two common traits appearing when the ten most valued traits perceived by the teachers of above schools were compared with those of experts nomination. The correlations between the rankings of the experts and teachers in four types of schools namely, Aided, Government, Kendriya and Public, are extremely low. From the results, it seems that the teachers of these schools according to criterion (evaluation against expert nomination) may be unduly punishing originality, individuality and spontaneity.

The results presented here in concerning the perception of the ideal pupils show that the teachers of four types of schools, namely,

Aided, Government, Kendriya and Public, have given a high place to characteristics such as courteous, doing work on time, remembering well, industrious, altruistic, obedient and self-confident — and a close agreement exists between the perception of teachers of the above schools on the qualities which they value most.

It is not difficult to speculate an explanation for such a phenomenon. Cultural conditions play an important role in enhancing or retarding the creative potential of children. Culture, as Teicher (1963) believes, is the matrix and the context of creativity; indeed it is the context for all the creative behaviours. So, if the teachers rank 'does work on time', 'courteous', 'obedient' etc. as important characteristics, there is nothing alarming in it. The whole fabric of the culture of India, is by and large, designed to emulate and prize the virtues of obedience. The various Indian religious texts, practices and customs highlight obedience to parents, elders and teachers as a quality to be developed among the children. And for 'Courteousness', Torrance writes that a creative child may be too busy to be courteous — if not too busy with his hands, too busy with the mind. Curious, searching has been looked on as a trait of creative person. Here in this study, curious gets first rank in Aided schools but is followed by courteous and healthy. In Government schools 'curious' follows 'remembering well' and is followed by 'doing work on time' and obedience. 'Curious' follows 'courteous', 'polite' and is followed by 'healthy' and 'remembering well' in Kendriya schools. In Public schools, 'curious' follows 'courteous', 'healthy' and is followed by 'doing work on time', 'altruistic' and remembering well. This, of course, looks somewhat incongruent.

The teachers of all four types of schools have placed being negativistic, talkative, disturbs, bashful, critical of others, fault-finding, spirited in disagreement and guessing as the characteristics which they value least. It may be observed that creative individuals are independent thinkers and this makes them negativistic and fault-finding. Since the creative individuals are skeptical, they are also critical and as a result of this attitude, they become unconventional and independent and consequently fault-finding with the statutory, customary and all that is accepted uncritically. Creative individuals at times may be bashful and timid as well. The characteristics which are not liked and valued least by the teachers of the schools are the ones which are considered important and necessary for creative accomplishments by the experts on creativity. From this, one gets the impression that the teachers of these four types of schools, namely, Aided, Government, Kendriya and Public impose sharp restraints on originality and creativity.

If the evaluation of the experts on creative personality is considered as the criterion, one will be discouraged to observe that the teachers of all the four types of schools, namely, Aided, Government, Kendriya and Public do not look favourably to the development of the creative potential and the tendency to explore and innovate. In fact, the characteristics which teachers of the above types of schools value most are the ones which experts on creative personality rate as the least valued. The correlations between the teachers' perception of these schools and the experts nomination as reported earlier are quite low indicating that teachers in general do not perceive creative behaviour and the qualities associated with it as something which should be encouraged and eulogised.

SECTION D

Socio-Economic Status and Creativity

Socio-economic status has been found to be a significant factor in most of the cognitive and psycho-motor performances. It enters although indirectly into the learning and is regarded to bear some relationship with creativity. The reason being that a family enjoying a high socio-economic status is able to provide for conditions and facilities conducive for the growth of creativity and vice-versa. Table 6.37 yields information in respect of socio-economic status of the subjects selected and studied in Aided, Government, Kendriya and Public schools and Table 6.38 about the relationship of creativity and socio-economic status.

Comparison of Socio-Economic Status of Students of Four Types of Schools

Mean, standard deviation values on socio-economic status of the students of four types of schools, and also *F* and *t*-values are presented in the Table 6.37.

TABLE 6.37: Means, S.D. and *t*-Values of Socio-Economic Status of Students of Four Types of Schools

Schools Type	Aided	Government	Kendriya	Public
Aided	$\bar{x}$ = 142.49 σ = 33.71	t = 0.80	t = 11.95**	t = 14.58**
Government	—	$\bar{x}$ = 145.65 σ = 30.62	t = 12.03**	t = 14.99**
Kendriya	—	—	$\bar{x}$ = 187.80 σ = 23.12	t = 2.85**
Public	—	—	—	$\bar{x}$ = 195.50 σ = 14.0

F-Value = 18.61**.

Table 6.37 reveals the following characteristics in regard to socio-economic status of the students of the four types of schools, namely, Aided, Government, Kendriya and Public:

1. Significant difference exists among students of the four types of schools (*F* = 118.61**) in respect of their socio-economic status.
2. Paired comparison of the socio-economic status of the students of schools reveal that:

   (i) The socio-economic status of students studying in Aided schools differ significantly from the socio-economic status of the students studying in Kendriya (*t*=11.95**), and Public schools (*t*=14.58**).

   (ii) No significant difference, however, has been observed in the socio-economic status of the students studying in Aided and Government schools (*t*=0.80).

   (iii) Students of Government schools differ significantly from the students of Kendriya schools (*t*=12.03**) and Public schools (*t*=14.99**) in respect of their socio-economic status.

   (iv) The socio-economic status of the students of Kendriya schools is significantly different from the socio-economic status of the students of Public schools (*t*=2.85**).

   (v) The students of Public schools have been found to have the best socio-economic status ($\bar{x}$=195.50), followed by Kendriya ($\bar{x}$=187.80), Government ($\bar{x}$=145.65) and Aided ($\bar{x}$=142.49).

(vi) There are much greater variations in the socio-economic status of the students studying in Aided schools (S.D. = 33.71) and much less in Public schools (S.D. = 14.00). The socio-economic status variations in Kendriya schools (S.D. = 23.12) are lesser to those observed in Government schools (S.D. = 30.62).

Relationship between Socio-Economic Status and Creativity

Table 6.38 records the co-efficient of correlation between socio-economic status and different forms of creativity in four types of schools.

TABLE 6.38: Correlation between Socio-economic Status of Students and Creativity in Four types of Schools and in Total Sample

Types of Schools	*r*-Values			
	Verbal Creativity (A)	Verbal Creativity (B)	Non-verbal Creativity	Total Creativity
Aided	0.253**	0.237**	0.198**	0.249**
Government	−0.059	−0.095	0.014	−0.072
Kendriya	−0.018	−0.028	−0.012	−0.025
Public	0.299**	0.241**	−0.043	0.172
Total Sample	0.092*	0.141**	0.225**	0.188**

The above table presents the following observations:

Socio-economic status, it seems, influences creativity. The magnitude of its influence on creativity, however, is rather modest. This is evident from the correlation value (r=0.188**) obtained between creativity and socio-economic status obtained on the basis of the sample undifferentiated into school types. The correlation value from the total sample of XI graders is not only significant in respect of socio-economic status and creativity but also in respect of its three types i.e. verbal creativity A (r=0.092*), verbal creativity B (r=0.141**) and non-verbal (r=0.225**).

The above observation holds completely true in the case of Aided schools and substantially in the case of Public schools. The reason being, socio-economic status is significantly correlated with total creativity (r=0.249**) and with all of its components, verbal creativity A (r=0.253**), verbal creativity B (r=0.237**) and non-verbal creativity (r=0.198**) in the Aided schools. In Public schools socio-economic status has been found to be significantly correlated with verbal creativity A (r=0.299**), and verbal creativity B (r=0.241**). No correlation between socio-economic status and creativity as well as its components has been found to be significant with samples from Government and Kendriya schools.

The above correlation values imply that the influence of socio-economic status on creativity and its components is just of marginal magnitude. Those who come from high socio-economic status have the added advantage of living in an environment pregnant with intellectual talks, critical academic exchanges, radio, television and other media leading to divergent thinking. Socio-economic status, thus, instead of entering directly into the phenomenon of creativity, enters indirectly through the afore-mentioned media. It should also be made clear at this stage that those who come from high socio-economic status will necessarily have the benefit of media encouraging the growth of creativity. There may be some parents even in low socio-economic status who in the interest of their wards may arrange conditions conducive for the growth of creativity. It is because of these situations that correlation between socio-economic status and creativity is rather low.

7

SUMMARY AND CONCLUSIONS

After interpreting the data and results in the preceding chapter, the chapter in hand proposes to present summary and conclusions which have been obtained in the study. It is further proposed to present the conclusions objectivewise. It will also be the effort of this chapter to throw light on the validity of the hypotheses presented in the fourth chapter of this book.

This study "Types of schools and corresponding factors as predictors of creativity at secondary level" was designed to examine the possible involvement of certain back-ground, organisational and environmental variables in the creative performance of students of four types of schools, namely, Aided, Government, Kendriya and Public. Type of school (administrative management basis) was taken as organisational variable, classroom climate and Teacher's perception of an ideal pupil were taken as environmental variables and socio-economic status of students was taken as background variable. Specifically the study tried to answer the following questions:

1. Do the students of four types of schools, namely, Aided, Government, Kendriya, and Public differ in level of creativity.
2. Does the classroom learning environment of the above schools differ.
3. Do the high and low creatives differ in their perceptions of classroom learning environment dimensions.
4. What is the relationship between classroom learning environment and creativity of the students in the four types of schools.
5. Do the dimensions of classroom learning environment predict creativity in the four types of schools and in total sample.
6. Do the teachers of the above four types of schools differ in their perceptions of an ideal pupil.

7. What is the relationship between teachers' perception and creative achievements of the students in the earlier mentioned schools.
8. Do the students of Aided, Government, Kendriya and Public schools differ in their socio-economic status.
9. What is the relationship between socio-economic status of students and their creativity in the above-mentioned schools.

The instruments used in this study were:

1. Verbal and Non-verbal tests of creativity by Dr. Baqer Mehdi.
2. Learning environment inventory by Gary J. Anderson and others.
3. Ideal pupil check-list by Dr. E. Paul Torrance.
4. Socio-economic status scale by Dr. S.P. Kulshreshtha.

The sample consisted of 480 male science student of class XI from 12 schools of Western Uttar Pradesh. These schools were selected from four types of schools, namely — Aided, Government, Kendriya and Public in equal number. Besides 275 teachers were selected from these different schools, who were given ideal pupil check-list to assess their perceptions about ideal pupil. The data were collected by administering verbal and non-verbal tests of creativity, Learning-environment Inventory and Socio-economic status scale to students of the above four types of schools.

The row scores of creativity were transformed into standard scores (*T*-scores) to make them comparable. The data, thus obtained were translated on data cards which were subjected to different statistical methods.

Mean and S.D. were calculated for all the variables under study. *F*-ratios were calculated to see overall difference in groups. *t*-test was applied to test the significance of difference in means. Product moment correlations were calculated to see the relationship between two variables. Besides rank order correlations were computed to study the agreement between the perception of teachers about ideal pupil in four categories of schools and experts' nomination. Stepwise multiple regression analysis of classroom learning environment dimensions was also done to see their predictive effectiveness in relation to creativity.

Based on the findings presented in the report, the following conclusions were derived.

School-wise Creativity Level of Students

The first objective with which the present study was initiated, was to find out and compare the XI graders of the four types of schools, namely, Aided, Government, Kendriya and Public in respect of verbal, non-verbal and total creativity and their components. The following are the conclusions drawn in respect to this objective:

1. XI graders have been found to have an average developed total creativity, verbal creativity (A and B) and their components and non-verbal creativity as well as its components.
2. Creativity and its components show variations in their development from school to school.
3. Although creativity and its components vary from school to school, the size of variation in the context of their mean score is small.
4. XI graders belonging to different schools namely, Aided, Government, Kendriya and Public differ in respect of the level of flexibility, originality, elaboration verbal, originality verbal, elaboration non-verbal, originality non-verbal, verbal creativity (A), verbal creativity (B), non-verbal creativity and total creativity.
5. XI graders of Aided schools differ in respect of their originality, elaboration verbal, originality verbal and verbal creativity (B) from the XIth graders of Government schools. They have also been found to differ significantly from students of Kendriya schools on creativity as well as such of its components as flexibility, originality, elaboration verbal, originality verbal, elaboration non-verbal and originality non-verbal, verbal creativity (A and B) and non-verbal creativity. Finally the students of Aided schools differ significantly in respect of the level of creativity and such of its components as elaboration verbal, originality verbal, originality non-verbal, verbal creativity (B) and non-verbal creativity from the students of public schools.
6. XI graders of Govt. schools differ significantly from students of Kendriya schools and public schools in respect of the growth of creativity as well as such of its components as originality non-verbal and non-verbal creativity. They

however, differ from students of Kendriya schools in respect of the growth of two such components as flexibility, elaboration non-verbal on which no such difference is found between them and the students of Public schools. However, originality verbal is the only creativity component on which they differ significantly from the students of Public schools.

7. Students of Kendriya Vidyalayas have been found to differ significantly from students of public schools on seven components of creativity namely, fluency, flexibility, originality, originality verbal, elaboration non-verbal, originality non-verbal and verbal creativity (A).
8. Students of Government schools are better than students of Aided schools on originality, elaboration verbal, originality verbal and verbal creativity (B).
9. Students of Kendriya Vidyalayas are even better than students of Govt. schools in respect of creativity and such of its components as flexibility, elaboration non-verbal, originality non-verbal and non-verbal creativity. In fact, they are not only better to students of Government schools but also to students of Public schools where teaching-learning process are considered to be of a high standard, on fluency, flexibility, originality, elaboration non-verbal and verbal creativity (A). As against the superiority of students of Kendriya Vidyalayas on over the students of public schools on the afore-mentioned five components, Verbal and non-verbal originality are the creativity components on which the students of Public schools show superiority over the students of Kendriya schools who as stated earlier generally excel over the students of other schools on creativity and a good number of its components.
10. Students of Kendriya Vidyalayas are found to be most creative, next in order are students of Public, Government and Aided schools.
11. The type of educational administrative set-up of a school is a significant factor in the growth of creativity. Each school offers an educational administrative set-up which is different from others. Administrative set-up in Kendriya schools seems to be more sensitive to the need for providing conditions for the growth of creativity. The efforts of Kendriya Vidyalayas get due rewards in the form of the growth of creative potential of their students.

The conclusions enumerated above reject the first null hypothesis substantially. There are, in fact significant differences among XI graders of the four types of schools in respect of total creativity, verbal and non-verbal creativity as well as several of their components. It is obvious from the conclusions stated above that the first objective of the study has been achieved beyond doubt.

Classroom Learning Environment in Four Types of Schools

The second objective of the study was to determine and compare the learning environment of Aided, Government, Kendriya and Public schools. Data obtained in this study has yielded the following conclusions in reference to this objective:

1. Learning environment of the four types of schools represented under such of its characteristics as cohesiveness, diversity, formality, speed, material environment, friction, goal direction, favouritism, difficulty, apathy, democracy, cliqueness, satisfaction, disorganisation, competitiveness and innovation does not show substantial differences. The quantum of variation too in each school is also rather small in the context of its mean score. Out of the sixteen characteristics of the learning environment, significant differences have been observed on nine of these, namely, cohesiveness, formality, speed, material-environment, goal-direction, difficulty, apathy, satisfaction and innovation among the four types of schools where and for which comparisons were made.
2. Aided schools differ from Government schools on one dimension of learning environment, namely material-environment, from Kendriya Vidyalayas on five dimensions namely, cohesiveness, formality, speed, material-environment and innovation and from public schools on six dimensions, namely, cohesiveness, formality, speed, goal-direction, difficulty and apathy.
3. Students of Government schools differ from students of Kendriya Vidyalayas on four dimensions of learning environment. These are cohesiveness, formality, speed, and material-environment. They have been found to differ significantly from students of public schools on as many as

seven components of learning environment. These are cohesiveness, formality, speed, material-environment, goal-direction, difficulty and apathy.

4. Students of Kendriya schools differ in respect of their perception of such characteristics of the learning environment as material-environment, goal-direction, difficulty, apathy and innovation from the perception of the students of public schools in this regard.
5. There is much greater cohesiveness in Kendriya schools in comparison to Aided and Government schools. However, public schools in this regard show as much cohesiveness as the Kendriya schools.
6. Aided schools stress on conformity to formal rules much more than the Government, Kendriya and the Public schools. In fact Public schools lay much less stress on conformity to the formal rules than the other institutions.
7. But for Aided and Government schools where there is almost and equal emphasis on the quickness of the completion of the courses, other institutions differ in this regard. Public schools make no effort to speedily complete their courses. But Aided schools are characteristically the institution which lay maximum stress on the speedy completion of the courses or class work.
8. Goal-direction is significantly much more manifest in Kendriya Vidyalayas than in other schools.
9. Students of Public schools perceive their learning tasks to be more difficult than is the perception of students of other schools in this regard.
10. Students of Public schools show more apathetic attitude towards class work than students studying in other institutions.
11. Innovation dimension is relatively much more manifest in Aided schools than in other schools.
12. All type of schools do not show distinctive differences in respect of such characteristics of learning environment as diversity, friction, favouritism, democracy, cliqueness, satisfaction, disorganisation and competitiveness.

Conclusions enumerated above substantially reject the null hypothesis framed in this study. The results show that the Aided, Government, Kendriya and Public schools differ significantly on many dimensions of learning environment. It is also evident that the differences among the schools are not uniform, on some dimensions of learning environment noticeable differences exist in some schools and on some others noticeable differences are observable in other institutions.

Conclusions enumerated earlier suggest that the second objective of the study has also been achieved.

Learning Environment Dimensions and Contrasting Groups of Creatives

The third objective with which the present study was initiated, was to compare high and low creatives of four types of schools and the total sample in respect of each one of the sixteen components of learning environment. Conclusions drawn after processing the data in this regard are as under:

1. The contrasting groups of high and low creatives of the four types of schools show significant differences on very few learning environment dimensions.
2. The high and low creatives of Aided schools differ only on the material-environment component of the learning environment. On the remaining fifteen learning environment dimensions, the contrasting groups do not differ.
3. The high and low creatives of Government schools differ on friction, difficulty and innovation components of learning environment.
4. The high and low creatives of Kendriya Vidyalayas do not differ on any of the sixteen dimensions of learning environment.
5. The high and low creatives of Public schools differ on three learning environment components namely, formality, favouritism and satisfaction.
6. The high and low creatives of the total sample differ significantly on two components of learning environment. These are speed and difficulty. The high creatives find that the speed of the completion of the class work and the difficulty of the class assignment is less than is the perception of the low creatives in this regard.

The conclusions enumerated above give ample support to the null hypothesis framed in this study. The high and low creatives either belonging to a specific type of school or belonging to the total sample have not been found to differ significantly on a good number of learning environment dimensions. Thereby implying that the perception of high and low creatives is almost alike on most of the learning environment dimensions.

Conclusions as above indicate clearly that the third objective of the study has been achieved.

Relationship between Learning Environment and Creativity

The fourth objective of the study was to find out the relationship between each one of the sixteen components of learning environment on the one hand and verbal creativity (A and B), non-verbal creativity and total creativity of the XI graders separately for each one of the above four types of schools as well as their total sample on the other.

Conclusions drawn in respect of this objective are as under:

1. Verbal creativity (A) has been found to be related with only one learning environment dimension, namely material-environment in Aided schools, with two dimensions: friction and innovation in Government schools, with competitiveness in Kendriya schools and with cohesiveness, friction, goal-direction, favouritism and competitiveness in Public schools and with friction, difficulty, competitiveness and innovation in the total sample.
2. The relationship between verbal creativity (A) on the one hand and above stated learning environment dimensions on the other in most of the cases is of a negative type.
3. Competitiveness, goal-direction and difficulty are the only components which bear a positive relationship with verbal creativity (A).
4. The degree of relationship between verbal creativity (A) and learning environment dimensions described earlier is low.
5. Verbal creativity (B) has been found to be related with only one learning environment dimension, namely, material-environment in Aided schools, with three dimensions: friction, difficulty and innovation in Government schools, with cliqueness and competitiveness in Kendriya schools, and with

cohesiveness and competitiveness in Public schools and with speed, friction, difficulty, competitiveness and innovation in the total sample.

6. Cohesiveness, competitiveness, cliqueness and difficulty are the only components which bear a positive relationship with verbal creativity (B).
7. The degree of relationship between verbal creativity (B) and learning environment dimensions described earlier is low, though significant.
8. Non-verbal creativity has been found to be related with three learning environment dimensions, namely, material-environment, difficulty and disorganisation in Aided schools, with only one dimension, namely friction in Government schools, with no dimension in Kendriya schools, with formality, goal-direction, satisfaction and disorganisation in Public schools and with formality and speed in the total sample.
9. Relationship between non-verbal creativity on the one hand and above stated learning environment dimensions on the other in most of the cases is of a negative type.
10. Difficulty and disorganisation are the only components which bear a positive relationship with non-verbal creativity.
11. The degree of relationship between non-verbal creativity and learning environment dimensions described earlier is low.
12. Total creativity has been found to be related with two learning environment dimensions, namely, material-environment and disorganisation in Aided schools, with four dimensions, namely, formality, friction, difficulty and innovation in Government schools, with only one dimension, namely, competitiveness in Kendriya schools, with satisfaction in public schools and with speed, difficulty, satisfaction and innovation in the total sample.
13. Total creativity is negatively related with most of the learning environment dimensions.
14. Formality, difficulty, disorganisation and competitiveness are the only components which bear a positive relationship with total creativity.
15. The degree of relationship between total creativity and learning environment dimensions described earlier is low, although significant.

Conclusions enumerated above lend reasonably good support to the null hypothesis which envisaged insignificant differences in the relationship between learning environment dimensions and creativity and its components. Out of 320 correlation values significant values have been observed only in 48. This implies that in majority of the cases the relationship is not significant.

It is evident from the conclusions presented above that the fourth objective of the study has also been achieved.

Creativity Prediction Effectiveness of Learning Environment Dimensions

The fifth objective of the study was to examine the prediction effectiveness of the different components of learning environment in respect of creativity. Conclusions drawn in references to this objective are as under:

1. There are very few learning environment dimensions which can predict creativity or its components. This is true for all the types of schools.
2. The prediction effectiveness of those learning environment components which were found to be significant, varies in degree from school to school.
3. A school has a distinctive learning environment and the effects of the latter on creativity and its components are also distinctive.
4. Regression co-efficients on learning environment dimensions are mostly negative. This holds true for creativity and all of its components in school types and in total sample.
5. The more the number of learning environment dimensions combinedly correlating with creativity or with any of its components, the higher is the correlation and *vice versa*.
6. There is a steady increment in the multiple correlation value (R) with addition of learning environment dimension successively.
7. Although the number of learning environment dimensions having significant regression co-efficient is rather small, yet it is these few dimensions which account for substantial amount of variance in the total variance.
8. The above observation holds true for school to school and also

for total sample of the study.

9. Material-environment, cliqueness and favouritism are learning environmental dimensions which have been found to be significant in predicting verbal creativity (A), verbal creativity (B), non-verbal creativity and total creativity in Aided schools. Besides these significant predictions of creativity and its components, disorganisation has also been found to have predictive significance in respect of non-verbal creativity and total creativity.
10. The set of environment dimensions in Government schools having the ability to predict is different from the set of learning environment factors found in Aided schools or for that reason any other school. This set consists of innovation, friction, speed, difficulty and formality as predictors of verbal creativity (A), verbal creativity (B), and total creativity. Besides being predicted by the above set of predictors verbal creativity (A) can also be predicted by cohesiveness and verbal creativity (B) and total creativity by favouritism learning environment dimension. Non-verbal creativity in Government schools can be predicted by friction, speed, favouritism and goal-direction component of learning environment.
11. Competitiveness, difficulty, cliqueness and cohesiveness have been found to predict verbal creativity (A) and verbal creativity (B) in Kendriya schools. Verbal creativity (B) besides being predicted by the afore-mentioned factors can also be predicted by friction in the above schools.
12. Innovation, cohesiveness and difficulty are the learning environment components which can predict non-verbal creativity in Kendriya Vidyalayas. Creativity of the students of these schools can be predicted by competitiveness, difficulty, friction, cliqueness, diversity and cohesiveness of learning environment dimensions.
13. Competitiveness, favouritism, satisfaction and friction are the factors which can predict verbal creativity (A) in Public schools. Verbal creativity (B) of the Public school students can be predicted by cohesiveness, satisfaction, favouritism, competitiveness and disorganisation. Non-verbal creativity of the students of these very schools can be predicted by five learning environment components, namely, disorganisation, favouritism, apathy, goal-direction and democracy. Finally,

total creativity of the students of Public schools can be predicted by such learning environment components as satisfaction, favouritism, competitiveness and disorganisation.

14. Competitiveness, friction, satisfaction, speed, difficulty and innovation are some such learning environment dimensions which can predict verbal creativity (A and B) of the total sample. Apathy and favouritism are some other factors which appear in addition to the above factors to predict verbal creativity (A) and diversity is a factor in addition to the above factors which can predict verbal creativity (B).
15. Speed, cliqueness, diversity and apathy are found to be predictors of non-verbal creativity of the total sample.
16. Difficulty, speed, friction, satisfaction, competitiveness, diversity, innovation and cliqueness are some such learning environment dimensions which can predict total creativity of the total sample.
17. Given the knowledge of learning environment characteristics, there is the possibility of predicting creativity and its components.

The conclusions enumerated above lead to the rejection of the null-hypothesis which stated that learning environment factors will not significantly predict the creativity or its components. Learning environment components do predict the growth of creativity. Of course, the degree of prediction of creativity by these factors is rather small.

The conclusion stated above show that the fifth objective of the study has been achieved.

Teachers' Perception about the Ideal Pupil in Different Types of Schools

The sixth objective of the study was to compare the teachers' perceptions of the ideal pupil in the four types of schools.

Conclusion drawn in respect of this objective is as under:

A high degree of association was found between the rankings and perceptions of teachers about the characteristics of an ideal pupil from different schools, namely, Aided, Government, Kendriya and Public. The teachers of four types of schools agreed to a very great extent on the type of qualities which they would like to encourage or discourage in their pupils.

In the context of above conclusion, it is evident that sixth objective has been achieved.

Relationship between Teachers' Perception and Creativity

The seventh objective of the study was to identify the relationship between Teachers' perceptions of an ideal pupil and creativity in each one of the four types of schools.

Conclusion drawn in respect of this objective is as below:

Very low association was found between the perception of teachers from four categories of schools namely, Aided, Government, Kendriya and Public and the ratings of experts on creative personality. According to this criterion (evaluation of teacher perception against expert nomination), it seems that teachers may be unduly punishing creativity, spontaneity and independence. Thus null hypothesis stands valid.

In the context of above conclusion, it is evident that the seventh objective of the study has been achieved.

Socio-economic Status of Students of different Types of Schools

The eighth objective of the study was to compare the students of Aided, Government, Kendriya and Public schools in respect of their socio-economic status. Conclusions drawn in respect of this objective are as under:

1. Students of Aided, Government, Kendriya and Public schools differ significantly in respect of their socio-economic status.
2. Most of the students of Public schools are drawn from families of high socio-economic status.
3. Students of the Aided schools are drawn from the families most of which belong to either low or middle socio-economic status.
4. Students of Government schools also happen to be drawn from families of socio-economic status similar to that of students of Aided schools.
5. Students of Kendriya Vidyalayas are also relatively from affluent section of society.
6. There are significant differences among students of different

schools in respect of their socio-economic status.

Conclusions enumerated above lead to rejection of null hypothesis framed in this study. There are very significant differences in the socio-economic status of students of different types of schools. As such null hypothesis stands rejected.

In the context of above conclusions, it is evident that the eighth objective of the study has been achieved.

Relationship between Socio-economic Status and Creativity

The final objective of the study was to identify relationship between socio-economic status of the students and their creativity in four types of schools and in total sample.

Conclusions drawn in respect of this objective are enumerated as below:

1. Socio-economic status influences creativity and its three types, namely, verbal creativity (A), verbal creativity (B) and non-verbal creativity significantly in Aided schools and in total sample. However neither creativity, nor its types have been found to be influenced significantly by socio-economic status in the remaining three types of schools, namely, Government, Kendriya and Public.
2. Socio-economic status influences creativity and its components to a moderate degree only.

Conclusions enumerated above lead us neither to accept nor to reject the null hypothesis convincingly. However in the context of total sample the trend appears to be more towards rejection of the null hypothesis than towards its acceptance.

It is obvious from the above that the ninth and final objective of the study has been achieved.

Educational Implications

They story of civilisation from stone-age to space-age is the story of man's creative imagination. Toynbee has rightly said "a few creative minds can make an enormous difference to civilisation".

On 1st May, 1986, addressing the 20th Convocation of

Kurukshetra University, the Chairman of University Grants Commission, Prof. Yash Pal said that knowledge was a never ending process. In the past knowledge meant learning what was learnt by the previous generations. Today one had to change this concept. Knowledge should mean not only being a 'Curator' but also a 'Creater'.

The destiny of a country is shaped in her classrooms. The classroom is an idea-centre, a place where students and teacher are excited about learning and open to experiences.

The classroom can be a most effective setting for 'surprises' for creativity as process. It can be the one place in our society where a person can explore and discover without the necessity of producing some thing new or novel.

Creativity in the classroom is not some thing that will just happen. Research indicates that the conditions for creative thinking — the environment — must be established by the teacher.

Many psychologists and educationists conceive creativity as a learned behaviour that can be practised and mastered through the usual procedures of teaching — learning process and through manipulation of environmental conditions (Guilford, 1952; Maltzman et al., 1960; Torrance 1962, 65; Parnes, 1976).

The present study tried to explore the possibility of developing creativity in the schools by examining the classroom learning environment of the four types of schools, namely, Aided, Government, Kendriya and Public, the teachers' attitude towards creativity by examining the teachers' perception of an ideal pupil and also the possible involvement of the socio-economic status of the students of these schools in their creative achievements.

The findings show that there is not much difference in the learning environment of these different types of schools, and its relationship with creativity is not high. Our results are in tune with the view of Vernon (1964), who in a review of Creativity and Intelligence commented: "I strongly suspect some schools do much more to stimulate and foster, or else to inhibit, creative talent than others".

The present study also indicated that there is very low relationship between teachers' perception of an ideal pupil and ratings of experts on creative personality. The teachers of all the four types of schools were found to put greater value to traits like obedience, doing work on time, remembering well, courteous, industrious, willingness to accept the judgement of authorities. They do not like and even want to discourage in their students such qualities as being adventurous, asking questions about puzzling things, being critical of others, guessing, liking to work alone, negativistic attitude, disturbing procedures and organisation of the group etc. In such a situation, we can imagine the fate of creativity and creative students.

These observations get corroborated with the earlier findings and reports of MacKinnon, 1959; Getzels and Jackson, 1962; and Torrance, 1963. According to MacKinnon report, creative research scientists recalled having been unhappy both at home and at school. Getzels and Jackson found that teachers preferred high IQ students, eventhough highly creative students achieved as well, scholastically. Working with elementary school children, Torrance also reported that the high IQ student was preferred and was better known by his teachers than the more creative student.

If a few teachers are enthusiastic to develop in their students creative talent, then the present system of education which puts emphasis on getting good grades in examination, heavy courses of study, text-books, and methods of teaching do not allow them to spare time for answering and encouraging students' unconventional questions and independent projects.

If we want to honour and develop the creative talents of our children and develop the country in turn, the whole system of education including courses of study, aims and objectives of education, text-books, examination system and teachers' selection procedures putting a great emphasis on their attitude towards teaching and development of creative talent and their training programmes needs almost overhauling and drastic changes.

If creativity is seen at some places in a few pupils, it is by chance. It is not deliberate and planned. So, if we want to keep pace with the most advanced countries of the world, then we have to plan a new system of education, in which creativity and creative pupils get honour, love and respect, and teachers find ample time, opportunities and encouragement for the development of creative potentials of their students and thereby changing classrooms as creative classrooms and teachers as nation-builders in the real sense of the term.

The Investigator would like to end the educational implications of this research study in the following words:

"A fair idea put to use is better than a good idea kept on the polishing wheel".

—Alex F. Osborn

Suggestions for Further Research

No investigation is worth the name which claims to be final, exhaustive and perfect. The present investigation, thus, opens doors and paves way for further research in the area of Creativity and Environment. Therefore, it would be in the fitness of things to suggest problems for further research. For further investigations, a few suggestions are given below:

1. The present study needs to be replicated on other grade levels such as primary, middle and lower secondary classes.
2. A study of Teachers' perception about ideal pupil can be done on primary and middle schools.
3. The present study can be done on students of different disciplines such as arts, commerce and professional courses like law, medical and engineering.
4. The present study needs to be replicated on the students of girls' schools.
5. A comparative study can be done on rural and urban schools regarding their classroom learning environment and its relationship with their students' creativity.
6. A comparative study of urban and rural school teachers can be done in regard to their perception about ideal pupil and its relationship with students' creativity.
7. A comparative study of boys and girls' schools can be done in regard to the classroom learning environment and teachers' perception of an ideal pupil.
8. A comparative study of different states can be done to study the creativity level of students, classroom learning environment, teachers' perception of the ideal pupil and socio-economic status of students.

BIBLIOGRAPHY

Anastasi, A. (Ed.). *Testing Problems in Perspective.* American Council on Education, Washington, D.C., 1966.

Anderson, G.J. and Walberg, H.J. 'Learning Environment'. In H.J. Walberg (Ed.) *Evaluating Educational Performance,* Berkeley : Mecutchan, 1974.

Anderson, G.J., Walberg, H.J. and Fraser, B.J. *Manual for Learning Environment Inventory (LEI),* Macquarie University, May, 1981.

Anderson, Harold H. (Ed.). *Creativity and its Cultivation*, New York: Harper and Row Publishers, 1959.

Argyris, Chris. *Organisation and Innovation*, Homewood, Illinois: Richard D. Irwin, Inc. and the Dorsey Press.

Badrinath, S. and Satyanarayan, S.B., 'Correlates of Creative Thinking of High School Students'. *Creativity News Letter,* 1979, 7 and 8, 2.

Barron, F. *Creative Person and Creative Process,* New York: Holt, Rinehart and Winston, 1969.

Baughman, M.D. and Eberle, R.E. 'The Open Classroom: Guidelines for the Creative Teacher'. *Clearing House,* March, 1965, pp. 387-392.

Best, J.W. *Research in Education.* Delhi: Prentice-Hall of India.

Biddle, B.J. 'The Institutional Context', in W.J. Campbell (Ed.) *Scholars in Context: The Effects of Environments on Learning,* Sydney: John Wiley and Sons, Pvt. Ltd., 1970.

Bloom, B.S. (1958). Quoted in R.L. Ebel (Ed.): *Encyclopaedia of Educational Research,* Fourth Edition, London: The Macmillan Co., 1969, p. 599.

Bock, R.D. *Multivariate Statistical Methods in Behavioural Research,* New York: McGraw-Hill Co., 1975.

Bruner, J.S. 'The Conditions of Creativity'. In H.E. Gruber, G. Terrell and M. Wertheimer (Eds.) *Contemporary Approaches to Creative Thinking,* New York: Atherton Press, 1962.

Buber, M. *Between Man and Man,* Boston: Beacon Press, 1961.

Buch, M.B. *A Survey of Research in Education*, Baroda: CASE, M.S. University, 1974.

Buch, M.B. *A Second Survey of Research in Education,* Baroda: CASE, M.S. University, 1979.

Buhl, H.R. *Creative Engineering Design,* Iowa State University Press, 1960.

Campbell, W.J. (Ed.) *Scholars in Context,* New York: John Wiley and Sons, 1970.

Chadha, N.K. and Sen, A.K. 'Creativity as a Function of Intelligence, Socio-economic Status and Sex Among 12th Grade School Students'. *Journal of Education and Psychology,* Vol. 39, No. 1, 1981, pp. 52-56.

Chambers, J.A. 'College Teachers: Their Effects on Creativity of Students'. *Journal of Educational Psychology,* Vol. 65, No. 3, 1973, pp. 326-334.

Chauhan, N.S. and Tiwari, G. *Manual of Creativity Test,* Agra: Agra Psychological Research Cell, 1974.

Chhaya, M.P. (1977). 'An Inquiry into the Achievement in Physics of Pupils of Class 8th and 10th of Schools belonging to Kendriya Vidyalaya Sangathan, Council of ISCE and All India Secondary Board'. *Second Survey of Research in Education,* 1979.

Christie, T. 'Environmental Factors in Creativity'. *The Journal of Creative Behaviour,* Vol. 4, 1970, pp. 13-31.

Christopher, James Kalvin, 'Teacher Perceptions of Factors in the School Environment which Influence Innovative Science Teaching'. *DAI,* 39, 6, Dec. 1978, p. 3495.

Cohen, L. *Educational Research in Classrooms and Schools,* London: Harper and Row Publishers, 1976.

Coleman, J.S. 'Social Climates in High School'. Cooperative Research Monograph No. 4, 1961.

Coleman, J.S. et al. *Equality of Educational Opportunity,* United States Deptt. of Health Education and Welfare, Washington D.C., 1966.

Covington, M.V. and Crutchfield. R.S. 'Facilitation of Creative Problem Solving'. *Programmed Instruction,* Vol. 4, No. 10, 1965, pp. 3-5.

Craig, R. 'Trait Lists and Creativity'. *Psychologia International Journal of Psychology,* Vol. 9, 1966, pp. 107-110.

Cropley, A.J. 'Creativity and Intelligence'. *British Journal of Educational Psychology,* Vol. 36, 1966, pp. 259-266.

Crutchfield, R.S. 'Conformity and Creative Thinking'. In H.E. Gruber, G. Terrell, and M. Wertheimer (Ed.) *Contemporary Approach to Creative Thinking,* New York: Atherton Press, 1962, pp. 120-140.

David, Thomas G., and Wright, Benjamin D. (Ed.) *Learning Environments,* Chicago: The University of Chicago Press, 1975.

Dehlevi, N. and Torrance, E.P. 'Iranian Mothers' Perception of the Ideal Child'. *Gifted and Talented Education,* 1979, 1, pp. 107-111.

Denny, David A. 'Identification of Teacher-Classroom Variables Facilitating Pupil Creative Growth'. *American Educational Research Journal,* Vol. 5, No. 3, May, 1968.

DeRoche, E.F. 'Creativity in the Classroom'. *Journal of Creative Behaviour,* Vol. 2, No. 4, 1968.

Dewey, J. 'Learning As Socialising'. In Vandenberg, D. (Ed.) *Teaching and Learning,* Urbana, IL: University of Illinois Press, 1969, p. 242.

Drevdahl, J.E. 'Factors of importance for Creativity'. *Journal of Clinical Psychology,* Vol. 12, 1956, pp. 21-26.

Drevdahl, J.E. 'Some Developmental and Environmental Factors in Creativity'. In C.W. Taylor (Ed.). *Widening Horizons in Creativity,* New York. John Wiley and Sons , Inc. 1964, pp. 170-185.

Dutta, N.K. and Gurbaksh Lal. *Creativity Potential and Education,* Ambala: Indian Book Agency, 1977.

Dye, M.E. 'An Enquiry into Creativity and its nurturing Climate : An Exploratory Study'. *The Journal of Creative Behaviour,* 1 (2), 1967, 208.

Ebel, R.L. (Ed.). *Encyclopaedia of Educational Research,* Fourth Edition, London: The Macmillan Co., 1969.

Eble, K.E. *A Perfect Education,* New York: Collier Books, 1968.

Feeley, J.T. 'Interest Patterns and Media Preferences of Boys and Girls in Grades Four and Five'. *DAI,* 1972, 33, pp. 108-190.

Ferguson, G.A. *Statistical Analysis in Psychology and Education,* (4th Ed.), New York: McGraw-Hill Book Co. 1976.

Foster, F.P. 'The Human Relationship of Creative Individuals'. *Journal of Creative Behaviour,* Vol. 2, No. 2, 1968.

Foster, J. *Creativity and the Teacher,* London: The Macmillan Co. Ltd., 1971.

Forehand, G.A. and Gilmer, B.V.H. 'Environmental Variation in Studies of Organisational Behaviour'. *Psychological Bulletin,* 1964, 62, pp. 361-384.

Fromm, Erich, 'The Creative attitude'. In Anderson, H.H. (Ed.). *Creativity and its cultivation,* New York: Harper and Brothers, 1959.

Garrett, H.E. *Statistics in Psychology and Education,* New York: David McKay Co. Inc., 1969.

Getzels, J.W. and Jackson, P.W. *Creativity and Intelligence: Explorations with Gifted Students,* New York: John Wiley and Sons, 1962.

Getzels, J.W. and Jackson, P.W. 'The Creative Adolescent- A Summary of Some Research Findings'. In C.W. Taylor (Ed.) *The Third University of Utah Research Conference on the Identification of Creative Scientific Talent',* University of Utah Press, 1959, pp. 46-57.

Getzels, J.W. and Jackson, P.W. 'Family Environment and Cognitive Style : A Study of the Sources of Highly Intelligent and Highly Creative Adolescents'. In Ross, L. Mooney and T.A. Razik (Ed.) *Explorations in Creativity,* New York: Harper and Row Publishers, 1967, 135-148.

Getzels, J.W. and Madaus, G.F. 'Creativity' in R.L. Ebel (Ed.). *Encyclopedia of Educational Research,* (IV Edition), London: The Macmillan Co., 1969.

Getzels, J.W. and Thelen, H.A. 'Classroom As a Social System-Dynamics of Instructional Groups', *Year Book of Education,* National Society for the Study of Education, 1960.

Ghiselin, B. (Ed.). *The Creative Process,* New York: Mentor Books, 1952.

Good, Carter V. *Dictionary of Education* (2nd Edition), New York: McGraw-Hill Book Co. Inc., 1959.

Gowan, J.C.; Demos D. George and Torrance, E. Paul (Eds.). *Creativity: Its Educational Implications,* New York: John Wiley and Sons, 1967.

Goyal, R.P. 'Creativity and School Climate An Exploratory Study'. *Journal of Psychological researches*, 1973, pp. 77-80.

Guilford, J.P. 'Creativity'. *American Psychologist,* Vol. 5, No. 9, 1950, pp. 444-454.

Guilford, J.P. 'The Structure of Intellect'. *Psychological Bulletin,* Vol. 53, 1956, pp. 267-293.

Guilford, J.P. 'Traits of Creativity'. In Vernon, P.E. (Ed.) *Creativity,* Suffolk, England: Penguin Books, 1970, p. 182.

Guilford, J.P. *Psychometric Methods* (2nd Ed.). New York: McGraw-Hill Book Co. Inc.

Guilford, J.P. 'Some Theoretical Views of Creativity' in H. Helson and W. Bevan (Eds.). *Contemporary Approaches to Psychology,* New York: Van Nostrand Reinhold Co. 1964b, pp. 419-459.

Guilford, J.P. 'Intellectual Factors in Productive Thinking' in R.L. Mooney and T.A. Razik (Eds.), *Explorations in Creativity,* New York: Harper and Row, 1967b.

Guilford, J.P. *Intelligence, Creativity and Their Educational Implications,* Sandiago, California: R.R. Knapp Publishers, 1968.

Guilford, J.P. 'A Letter to S.J. Parnes' quoted in C.W. Taylor (Ed.) *Climate for Creativity: Report of the Seventh National Research Conference on Creativity,* New York: Pergamon Press Inc., 1972, p. 196.

Guilford, J.P. and Merrifield, P.R. 'The Structure of Intellect Model: its Uses and Implications'. Reports from the Psychological Laboratory, No. 24, Los Angeles: University of Southern California, 1960.

Gupta, A.K. 'Creativity Research in India: Its Past and Future'. *Creativity News Letter,* 3(1), 1974, pp. 18-24.

Gupta, A.K. 'Identifying Environmental Factors in Creativity'. *Creativity News Letter,* Vol. 5, No. 2, 1976, pp. 38-49.

Gupta, A.K. 'A Study of Pupil Creativity in Two Institutional Environments'. *The Journal of Creative Behaviour,* 1977.

Haddon, F.A. and Lytton, H. 'Teaching Approach and the development of Divergent Thinking Abilities in Primary Schools'. *British Journal of Educational Psychology,* Vol. 38, 1968, pp. 171-180.

Haddon, F.A. and Lytton, H. 'Primary Education and Divergent Thinking Abilities'. *British Journal of Educational Psychology,* 1971, pp. 136-147.

Hallman, R.J. 'The Necessary and Sufficient Conditions of Creativity'. *Journal of Humanistic Psychology,* 3:1, 1963.

Harrison, J.B., 'Variables of Home Environment Associated with Creativity in Children'. 1972, *DAI,* 33, 3918-B.

Hughes, M.M. 'Integrity in Classroom Relationship'. In Alice Miel (Ed.) *Creativity in Teaching,* Balmont, California: Wadsworth Publishing Co. Inc., 1962, pp. 41-70.

Jarial, G.S. 'Verbal Creative Thinking Among the Students with Different Socio-economic Status and Birth Orders'. *Psycho-Lingua,* Vol. 9, No. 2, 1979, pp. 85-90.

Kagan, J. (Ed.) *Introduction: Creativity and Learning,* Boston: Beacon Press, 1968.

Karlins, M. and Schroder, H.M. 'Discovery Learning: Creativity and Inductive Teaching Programme'. *Psychological Reports,* Vol. 20, No. 3, 1967.

Kendall, M.G. *A Course in Multivariate Analysis,* London: Charles Griffin and Co., 1957.

Kneller. G.F. *The Art and Science of Creativity,* New York: Holt, Rinehart and Winston Inc., 1965.

Kothari, D.S. *Report of the Education Commission,* Ministry of Education, Govt. of India, New Delhi, 1966.

Kratz, H.E. 'Characteristics of the Best Teachers as Recognised by the Children'. *Pedagogical Seminary,* 3, pp. 413-18, 1896.

Kulshreshtha, S.P. *Manual of Socio-economic Status Scale,* Agra: National Psychological Corporation, 1980.

Kundley, M.B. 'A Test of Literary Creativity in Marathi'. Doctoral Thesis, Nagpur University, Nagpur, 1977.

Kurtz, A.K. and Mayo, S.T. *Statistical Methods in Education and Psychology,* New York: Springer International Student, Edition, 1979.

Lasswell, H.D. 'The Social Setting of Creativity'. In H.H. Anderson (Ed.) *Creativity and Its Cultivation,* New York: Harper and Row, 1969, pp. 203-221.

Lefrancois, G.R. 'Psychology for Teaching: A Bear Always Faces the Front'. Belmont, California: Wadsworth Publishing Co. Inc., 1972.

Lemire. 'Creativity and School: A Social Problem'. *The Alberta Journal of Educational Research,* 1972, 18, 4.

Lowenfeld, V. and Brittain, W.L. *Creative and Mental Growth* (4th Ed.), New York: Macmillan, 1964.

Lytton, H and Cotton, A.C. 'Divergent Thinking Abilities in Secondary Schools'. *British Journal of Educational Psychology,* 1969, pp. 188-90.

MacKinnon, D.W. 'The Nature and Nurture of Creative Talent', *American Psychologist,* Vol. XVII, 1962, pp. 484-495.

MacKinnon, D.W. 'Identifying and Developing Creativity'. *Journal of Secondary Education,* 1963, 38, pp. 166-174.

MacKinnon, D.W. 'Creativity: A Multi-faceted Phenomenon'. In John D. Rosalnsky (Ed.). *Creativity,* Amsterdam: North-Holland Publishing Co., 1970.

Marjoribanks, K. 'Environment, Social Class and Mental Ability'. *Journal of Educational Psychology,,* 1972, 63, pp. 103-109.

Majumdar, S.K. *Scientific Creativity,* New Delhi: N.C.E.R.T. 1973, (Mimeographed).

Mansfield, R.S. and Busse, T.V. 'Theories of Creativity'. *Journal of Creative Behaviour,* 1980, 14, 2, pp. 91-103.

Mead, Margaret. 'Creativity in Cross Cultural Perspective', in H.H. Anderson (Ed.) *Creativity and its Cultivation,* New York: Harper and Row, 1959.

Marburg, G.S. 'The Relationship between classroom Climate and Creative performance among 5th grade Elementary School Children'. *D.A.I,* 1971, 31, 12A, p. 6407.

Martin, L.J. 'Psychological Investigations in Creativity: A Bibliography (1954-1965)'. *Research in Education* (ERIC), Vol. 3, No. 8, 1968.

Maslow, A.H. 'The Creative Attitude', in R.L. Mooney and T.A. Razik (Eds.) *Explorations in Creativity,* New York: Harper and Row Publishers, 1967.

Maslow, A.H. 'Creativity in Self-actualising People'. In H.H. Anderson (Ed.), *Creativity and its cultivation,* New York: Harper and Row Publishers, 1959.

Maslow, A.H. 'Emotional Blocks to Creativity'. *Journal of Individual Psychology,* 1958, 14, pp. 51-56.

Maslow, A.H. *Towards a Psychology of Being,* New York: D. Van Nostrand Co, Inc., 1962.

Maslow, A.H. *Motivation and Personality,* New York: Harper and Row Publishers, 1954 (Second Edition 1970).

Massialas, B.G. and Jevin, Jack. *Creative Encounters in the Classroom,* New York: John Wiley and Sons Inc., 1967.

May, Rollo. 'The Nature of Creativity'. In H.H. Anderson (Ed.), *Creativity and its Cultivation,* New York: Harper and Row, 1959.

McDaniel, E.R. 'An Investigation of the Relationship between Creativity and Socio-economic Status, Race and Sex of the Seventh Grade Pupils'. *DAI,* 1974, 34, 7A, pp. 3997-3998.

McPherson, L.C. *Definitions and Criteria of Creativity,* Midland: The Dow Chemical Co., 1960 (Mimeographed).

Mehdi, B. *Manual of Non-verbal Test of Creative Thinking,* Aligarh, 1973.

Mehdi, B. *Manual of Verbal Test of Creative Thinking*, Aligarh, 1973.

Mehdi, B. 'Creativity Teaching and Learning-Report', RCE, Mysore, 1977.

Misra, K.S. 'Anti-Creativity Climate'. *Creativity News Letter,* Vol. 7, No. 2, and Vol. 8, No. 1, 1979, pp. 41-43.

Mooney, R.L. and Razik, T.A. *Explorations in Creativity,* New York: Harper and Row, 1967.

Moos, R.H. 'Conceptualisations of Human Environments'. *American Psychologist,* 28, 1973, pp. 652-664.

Morrison, Harriet B. 'The Creative Classroom'. *Journal of Creative Behaviour*, Vol. 7, No. 3, 1973.

Moustakas, C.E. *Creativity and Conformity,* Princeton, New Jersey: D. Van Nostrand Company Inc., 1967.

N.C.E.R.T. The Curriculum for the Ten Year School : A Framework, New Delhi, N.C.E.R.T., 1975.

Nie, N.H. *Statistical Package for Social Sciences* (SPSS), (2nd Ed.), New York: McGraw-Hill Book Co., 1975.

Nogrady, 'An Investigation of the Relation between Open Structure Education and the Development of Creativity in Young Children'. *DAI,* 1976, 36, 11A, pp. 7304-7305.

Ogletree, E.J. 'A Cross Cultural Examination of the Creative Thinking Abilities of Public and Private School Pupils in England, Scotland and Germany'. *Journal of Social Psychology,* 83, 1971, pp. 301-302.

Osborn, A.F. *Applied Imagination,* New York: Charles Scribner's Sons, 1953.

Pachaury, A.C. 'Science Student Teachers' Perception of Ideal Pupil'. *Educational Trends,* 8, 1973, pp. 157-168.

Pachaury, A.C. 'Teachers' Perception of Creative Pupils'. *Creativity News Letter,* Vol. 3, No. 2, and Vol. 4, No. 1, 1975, pp. 38-39.

Pareek, U. and Rao, T.V. *Handbook of Psychological and Social Instruments,* Ahmedabad, 1974.

Parloff, M.B. and Morris, B. 'Creativity Research Programme : A Review'. In C.W. Taylor (Ed.). *Climate for Creativity,* New York: Pergamon Press Inc., 1972.

Parnes, S.J. 'Education and Creativity'. *Teachers College Record,* 1963-64, 1, pp. 331-339.

——— *Creative Behaviour Guide Book,* New York: Charles Scribner's Sons Inc., 1967 b.

Parnes, S.J. 'Methods and Educational Programmes for Stimulating Creativity: A Representative List'. *Journal of Creative Behaviour,* Vol. 2, No. 1, 1967.

——— 'Creativity Development' in S.E. Goodman (Ed.) *Handbook on Contemporary Education,* New York: A Zerox Education Co., 1976.

——— and Brunelle, E.A. 'The Literature of Creativity. *Journal of Creative Behaviour,* Vol. 1, No. 1, 1967.

——— and Harding, H.F. (Ed.). *A Source Book for Creative Thinking,* New York: Charles Scribner's Sons Inc., 1962.

Passi, B.K. *Creativity in Education,* Agra: National Psychological Corporation, 1982.

Phatak, P. *Your Ideal Student,* Baroda: M.S. University of Baroda, 1963.

Piaget, J. *Play, Dreams and Imitation in Childhood,* New York: Norton and Norton, 1962.

Pillay, G.S. 'Effects of Patterns of Teaching Upon Creative Thinking Among Adolescents'. *Teacher Education,* Vol. XI, No. 4, and Vol. XII, No. 1, 1977, pp. 27-40.

Pillay, J.K. 'Organisational Climate and Innovative Ability of schools'. *Quest in Education,* 12(2) 1975, pp. 104-111.

Popham, W.J. *Educational Statistics—Use and Interpretation,* New York: Harper and Row Publishers, 1967.

Raina, M.K. 'A Study into the Effect of Competition on Creativity'. *Gifted Child Quarterly,* 12(4) 1968, pp. 217-270.

——— 'An Exploratory Study of School Climate and Creativity'. *Indian Educational Review,* 1969 b.

——— 'Creativity Research in India: An Analysis'. *Journal of Creative Behaviour,* 1969, pp. 200-210.

——— 'Prospective Science Teachers' Perceptions of the Ideal Pupil'. *Journal of Research in Science Teaching,* 7, 1970, pp. 169-172.

——— 'A Review of Research on Creativity Functioning in India'. *Indian Educational Review,* 6(2), 1971, pp. 260-281.

——— *Creativity Research: International Perspective,* New Delhi: N.C.E.R.T., 1980.

Raina, T.N. and Raina, M.K. 'Perception of Teacher Educators in India About the Ideal Pupil'. *Journal of Educational Research,* 1971, pp. 303-306.

Ramey, C.T. and Piper, V. 'Creativity in Open and Traditional Classroom'. *Child Development,* 45, 2, 1974, pp. 557-560.

Randhawa, B.S. and Fu, L.L.W. 'Assessment and Effect of Some Classroom Environment Variables'. *Review of Educational Research,* Vol. 43, No. 1-4, 1973, pp. 303-323.

Rao, T. Venkateswara. 'Research on Institutional Environment: A Review'. *Indian Educational Review,* Vol. 6, No. 1, 1971.

Razik, T.A. 'Bibliography of Creativity Studies and Related Areas'. *Research in Education* (ERIC), Vol. 3, No. 8, 1968.

Rhodes, M. 'An Analysis of Creativity'. *Phi Delta Kappa,* 1961, 42, p. 305.

Rogers, C.R. 'Towards A Theory of Creativity'. In P.E. Vernon (Ed.). *Creativity,* Suffolk England: Penguin Books, 1970, p. 139.

——— *On Becoming a Person,* Boston: Houghton Mifflin Co., 1961.

——— 'Toward a Theory of Creativity', in H.H. Anderson (Ed). *Creativity and its Cultivation,* New York: Harper and Row Publishers, 1959.

Rogers, D.W. 'Visual Expression, A Creative Advantage of the Disadvantaged'. *Elementary School Journal,* 68, 1968, pp. 394-399.

Rossman, J. *The Psychology of the Inventor,* Washington: Inventor's Publishing Co., 1931.

Rousseau, H.J. 'Ability in a Multi-cultural Community'. In G.S. Bereday and J.A. Lauwerys (Eds), *The Year Book of Education,* London: Evan Brothers, 1962.

Ruedi, J. and West, C.K. 'Pupil Self-Concept in an open School and in a Traditional School'. *Psychology in the Schools,* 10, 1973, pp. 48-53.

Sachdeva, M. 'Learning and Socio-Emotional Climate of the Class: A Study'. *Educational Trends,* 1-2:3, 1969, pp. 15-19.

Sharma, K. 'A Study of Creativity with Certain Background, Psychological and Organisational Factors Among Students of Higher Secondary Schools of Delhi'. Doctoral Thesis, Faculty of Education, Jamia Millia Islamia, 1982.

Shukla, R.P. 'A Creative Attitude Test for Teachers' *Creativity News Letter,* 2(2), A.M.U., Aligarh, 1973, pp. 33-38.

Singh, R.P. 'A Study of Socio-Emotional Climate of the Classes of Higher Secondary Schools of Ajmer Distt.' *The Rajasthan Board J. of Secondary Education,* 1973, 8-3, pp. 60-63.

Skager, R.W., Schultze, C.B. and Klein, S.P. 'Quality and Quantity of Accomplishment as Measures of Creativity', *Journal of Educational Psychology,* 56, 1965, pp. 37-39.

Stein, M.I. 'Creativity and Culture'. *J. of Psychology,* 1953, 36, pp. 311-322.

Stein M.I. and Heinze, S.J. *Creativity and the Individual,* Glencoc, Illinois: Free Press, 1960.

Steele, J.M., House, E.R., and Kerins, T. 'An instrument for Assessing Instructional Climate through Low-Inference Student Judgements.' *American Educational Research Journal,* 8, No. 3, 1971, pp. 447-66.

Stern, G.G., Stein, M.I. and Bloom, B.S. *Methods in Personality Assessment,* Glencoe, Illinois: Free Press, 1956.

Sultana Ahmed. Effect of Socio-Cultural disadvantage on Creative Thinking. *Journal of Psychological Researches,* Vol. 24, No. 2, 1980, pp. 96-106.

Taylor, C.W. *Climate for Creativity,* Report of the Seventh National Research Conference on Creativity. New York: Pergamon, 1972.

Taylor, Calvin W. (Ed.) *Creativity: Progress and Potential,* New York: McGraw-Hill, 1964A.

Taylor, C.W. (Ed.) *Widening Horizons in Creativity,* New York: John Wiley, 1964b.

Taylor, C.W. and Barron, F. *Scientific Creativity: Its Recognition and Development,* New York: John Wiley and Sons, Inc., 1963.

Taylor, C.W. and Williams, F.E. *Instructional Media and Creativity,* New York: John Wiley and Sons Inc., 1966.

Taylor, P.H. 'Children's evaluation of the characteristics of a good teacher'. *British Journal of Educational Psychology,* 23, 1962, pp. 258-66.

Thangam, N. 'An Experimental Study of Classroom Climate'. Ph.D. Thesis, M.S. University, Baroda, 1980.

Tiwari, G. and Pal, Roma. *Status of Indian Researches in Creativity,* Agra: Agra Psychological Research Cell, 1983.

Torrance, E.P. 'The Creative Personality and the Ideal Pupil'. *Teachers College Record,* 1963, 65, pp. 220-226.

——— 'What kind of person do you want your gifted child to become?' *Gifted Child Quarterly,* 1963, 7, pp. 87-91.

——— What kind of people do we want gifted students to become? *High School Journal,* 1964, 48, pp. 88-93.

——— *Guiding Creative Talent,* Englewood cliffs N.J.: Prentice-Hall, 1962 (Indian Reprint, 1969).

——— 'Must creative development be left to chance?' *Gifted Child Quarterly,* 6, 1962, pp. 41-44.

Torrance, E.P. *Education and the Creative Potential,* Minneapolis: The University of Minnesota Press, 1963.

——— *Rewarding Creative Behaviour,* Englewood Cliffs, N.J.: Prentice Hall, 1965.

——— *Creativity,* Belmont, CA: Fearon Publishers, 1969, VIII.

——— 'What is honoured: Comparative Studies of Creative Achievements and Motivation'. *Journal of Creative Behaviour,* 1969.

——— *Encouraging Creativity in the Classroom,* Dubuque, Iowa: W.C. Brown Co., 1970.

——— *Manual Ideal Child Check List,* Georgia Studies of Creative Behaviour, Athens, Georgia, June 1975.

——— 'Towards the More Humane Education of Gifted Children'. *Gifted Child Quarterly,* 7, 1963, pp. 135-145.

——— and Myers, R.E. *Creative Learning and Teaching,* New York: D. Mead Co., 1970.

Toynbee, A. 'Has America Neglected Her Creative Minority'. In C.W. Taylor (Ed.), *Widening Horizons in Creativity,* New York: John Wiley and Sons, 1964.

Treffinger, D.J.; Ripple, R.E. and Dacey, J.S. 'Teachers' Attitudes About Creativity'. *The Journal of Creative Behaviour,* Vol. 2, 1967-68, p. 242.

Trickett, E.J. and Moos, R.H. 'Social Environment of Junior High and High School Classrooms'. *Journal of Educational Psychology,* 65, No. 1, 1973, pp. 93-102.

Trickett, E.J. and Moos, R.H. *Assessment of the Psycho-social Environment of the High School Classrooms,* Stanford, California : Stanford University School of Medicine, 1971.

Tuckman, B.W. et al. 'Evaluating the open classroom'. Paper presented at the meeting of the American Educational Research Association, New Orleans, April, 1973.

Verma, Lokesh K. 'A Study of Locus of Control of High and Low Creative High School Students At Different Socio-Economic Status'. *Indian Journal of Educational Psychology,* No. 2, 1980.

Vernon, P.E. (Ed.) *Creativity,* Suffolk, England: Penguin Books, 1970.

Vernon, P.E. 'Creativity and Intelligence', *Journal of Educational Research,* 1964, 6, pp. 163-169.

Vijai Lakshmi. 'Academic Achievement and Socio-economic Status as Predictors of Creative Talent'. *Journal of Psychological Researches,* Vol. 24, (1) 1980.

Visher, S.S. 'Environmental Background of Leading American Scientists'. *American Sociological Review,* 1948, 13, pp. 65-72.

Walberg, H.J. 'Structural and Affective Aspects of Classroom Climate'. *Psychology in Schools,* 5, 1968, pp. 247-253 b.

——— 'Teacher Personality and Classroom Climate'. *Psychology in Schools,* 5, 1969, pp. 163-169 b.

——— 'Social Environment as a Mediator of Classroom Learning'. *Journal of Educational Psychology,* 60, 1969, pp. 443-448 b.

——— (Ed). *Evaluating Educational Performance,* Berkeley, McCutchan, 1974.

——— and Anderson, G.J. 'The Achievement- Creativity Dimension and Classroom Climate'. *The Journal of Creative Behaviour,* Vol. 2, No. 4, 1968, pp. 281-292.

——— and Anderson, G.J. 'Classroom Climate and Individual Learning'. *Journal of Educational Psychology,* 1968, 59, pp. 414-419.

——— and Anderson, G.J. 'Assessing Classroom Learning Environments', in Marjoribanks, K. (Ed.), *Environments for Learning,* Slough, N.F.E.R. 1974.

——— and Singh, R. 'Teacher Quality Perceptions and Achievement in Rajasthan'. *The Alberta Journal of Educational Research,* Vol. XX, No. 3, 1974.

———, Singh, R. and Rasher, S.P. 'Predictive Validity of Learning Environment Inventory'. *American Educational Research Journal,* 14, No. 1, 1977, pp. 45-49.

——— and Thomas, S.C. 'Open Education : An Operational definition in Great Britain and United States'. *American Educational Research Journal,* 9, 2, 1972, pp. 197-208.

Walker, W.J. 'Creativity and High School Climate'. In J.C. Gowan, C.D. Demos and E.P. Torrance (Eds.), *Creativity: Its Educational Implications,* New York: John Wiley and Sons, 1967.

——— 'Teacher Personality in Creative School Environments'. *Journal of Educational Research,* 62, 1969, pp. 243-246.

Wallas, Graham. *The Art of Thought,* London: Watts, 1926.

Ward, W.C. 'Creativity and Environment. Cues in Nursery School Children'. *Developmental Psychology,* 1, 1969, pp. 543-47.

Weber, M.J. Perception of Human, Intermediate and Non-human classroom environments as viewed by VIII grade students. *DAI,* 38 : 10, April 1978, p. 5967.

Weber, W.M. 'Teacher Behaviour and Pupil Creativity'. *Dissertation Abstract International,* 29, 1967, p. 159.

Webster, Noah. *Webster's New Twentieth Century Dictionary,* Second Edition, Unabridged, Collins and World Publishing Co. Inc., 1977.

Weisberg, P.S. and Springer, K.J. 'Environmental Factors in Creative Function- A Study of Gifted Children'. *Archives of General Psychiatry,* 1961, pp. 554-64.

Wiesner, J.B. 'Education for Creativity in the Sciences', in Kagan, J. (Ed.), *Creativity and Learning,* Boston: Beacon Press, 1968, p. 96.

William, F.E. 'Models for Encouraging Creativity in the Classroom by Integrating Cognitive-Affective Behaviours'. *Educational Technology,* 1969, 9, pp. 7-13.

William, F.E. *Creativity at Home and in School,* Minnesota: Macalester Creativity Project, 1968.

Wilson, R.C. 'A Factor-Analytic Study of Creative Thinking Abilities. *Psychometrica,* 19, 1954, pp. 297-311.

Withal, J. 'The Development of Technique for the measurement of Socio-emotional Climate in Classroom'. *Journal of Experimental Education,* 17, 1949, pp. 347-361.

Withal, J. 'Evaluation of classroom Climate'. *Childhood Education,* March, 1969.

Wolf, R. 'The Measurement of Environments'. In Anastasi, A. (Ed.), *Testing Problems in Perspective,* A.C.E. Washington, D.C., 1966.

Yashpal, Kurukshetra University Convocation Lecture. *Hindustan Times,* 2nd May, 1986.

INDEX